BARE KNUCKLES

&

SARATOGA RACING

BARE KNUCKLES

&

SARATOGA RACING

THE REMARKABLE LIFE
=== OF ===
JOHN MORRISSEY

BRIEN BOUYEA

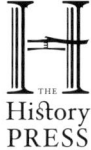

Published by The History Press
Charleston, SC
www.historypress.net

Copyright © 2016 by Brien Bouyea
All rights reserved

First published 2016

Manufactured in the United States

ISBN 978.1.46713.558.0

Library of Congress Control Number: 2016930763

Notice: The information in this book is true and complete to the best of our knowledge. It is offered without guarantee on the part of the author or The History Press. The author and The History Press disclaim all liability in connection with the use of this book.

All rights reserved. No part of this book may be reproduced or transmitted in any form whatsoever without prior written permission from the publisher except in the case of brief quotations embodied in critical articles and reviews.

For my parents, Thomas D. Bouyea and Pam O'Brien Bouyea

CONTENTS

Foreword, by Michael Veitch	9
Acknowledgements	11
Hope and Dreams	13
New York	23
Old Smoke	31
California Adventures	41
The American Champion	49
Streets of Blood	63
Fight of the Century	75
A Letter from Saratoga Springs	83
They're Off at Saratoga!	95
The Honorable John Morrissey	107
Epilogue: The Legacy of Old Smoke	123
Bibliography	135
Index	137
About the Author	141

FOREWORD

No individual in the rich history of Saratoga Springs, New York, created a taproot institution as deep as John Morrissey's iconic and enduring Saratoga Race Course.

In this biography of the celebrated track founder, author Brien Bouyea journeys through the extraordinary life of this unique nineteenth-century character, whose experiences made him perhaps the only person who could have established and developed elite racing at the Spa.

Morrissey organized and supported the inaugural thoroughbred race meeting in Saratoga Springs. It took place on the Saratoga Trotting Course in 1863, just a few weeks after the Battle of Gettysburg.

The circumstances of the Civil War should have worked against the success of a start-up venture in horse racing. Yet, in just two years, this champion prizefighter, gambler and future politician managed to have his new track, which opened in 1864, compared to the famous English courses of Ascot and Goodwood, which dated to 1711 and 1802, respectively.

Morrissey was able to pull together the men and money necessary to establish Saratoga as a national leader at the start. Saratoga played a leading role in the revival of thoroughbred racing in the wake of the sport's destruction at racing centers in the South.

Indeed, it can be said that with Morrissey at the helm, Saratoga helped in the nation's healing as a place where, despite the bitterness of the post–Civil War years, racing men from southern states traveled to his track for the summer season.

FOREWORD

There was concern about Morrissey's venture. Now that gambling and racing were underway, would the hotels attract the same genteel patrons as before the Civil War?

Morrissey instinctively knew how to chart the course. He personally maintained order at the track, moving about the stands to make sure good taste and behavior were upheld. In town, Morrissey proved to be a generous benefactor, establishing a custom of donating proceeds from racing days to local schools. He also made sure that such generosity extended to local churches and various other civic needs.

Morrissey is a precious gem in the city's history of notable and charismatic figures. The list includes Gideon Putnam, one of the founders of the Spa; Richard Canfield, who came to own Morrissey's Club House in Congress Park; actress and singer Lillian Russell; industrialist John "Bet-a-Million" Gates; and financier "Diamond" Jim Brady. Morrissey, rightfully so, belongs in such company.

On May 1, 1878, John Morrissey died at the Adelphi Hotel on Broadway in Saratoga Springs. He was forty-seven years old. That summer, a horse named Duke of Magenta won the Travers, Sequel, Kenner and Harding stakes at the Spa, following earlier victories in the Preakness, Belmont and Withers. It was the kind of horse Morrissey attracted to Saratoga from the start, followed by other giants named Hindoo, Man o' War, Whirlaway and Secretariat.

If there is a track today that has a place in the mind of the national sports fan, it is Saratoga, the one Morrissey founded and directed toward prosperity. In his short life, he could not have envisioned what it became.

Or maybe he could have.

MICHAEL VEITCH

ACKNOWLEDGEMENTS

Throughout the process of writing this biography of John "Old Smoke" Morrissey, I was constantly reminded of how blessed I am to have such an outstanding support system both in this endeavor and in life.

First, I would like to thank Michael Veitch, an expert on all matters pertaining to thoroughbred racing and the lead writer on the sport for the *Saratogian* since 1979. Always an accessible and gracious source of information and advice, Michael kindly agreed to make a significant contribution to this work by writing a foreword that provides essential perspective of Morrissey's legacy in Saratoga Springs, New York. As the dean of turf writers covering Saratoga Race Course, Michael has produced compelling stories about America's greatest racetrack in five decades. He is one of the most knowledgeable historians in the sport and a credit to Saratoga Springs.

The staff at the National Museum of Racing and Hall of Fame deserves recognition for both encouraging this book and the outstanding job it does every day of preserving and promoting the history of American racing. Chris Dragone, the museum's executive director, effectively leads a passionate and talented staff that I am honored to be a part of as director of communications. A special thanks goes to Victoria Tokarowski, the museum's curator, for helping locate several key images that enhance this work. I am also thankful to museum historian Al Carter for researching some pesky details that go back 150 years or so. Al ranks right up there with Michael Veitch among the most knowledgeable historians in racing.

At the Saratoga Springs History Museum, John Morrissey's former Saratoga Club House, executive director Jamie Parillo has been another

ACKNOWLEDGEMENTS

enthusiastic advocate of this project and provided access to the important George S. Bolster photographic collection. The History Museum is an essential destination for anyone interested in Morrissey and all other narratives relating to Saratoga Springs.

In Troy, New York, where Morrissey spent his formative years, I thank two people from my early days as a journalist at the *Record* newspaper. Without the guidance of Lisa Robert Lewis and Kevin Moran, there is no way I would be in the position I am today. Lisa, who recently retired after forty years at the paper, welcomed me with open arms as an intern on the news desk while I was studying at the College of Saint Rose in nearby Albany. I didn't know half as much as I thought I did, and Lisa put up with me nonetheless. Her door was always open whenever I had a question or needed direction. Perhaps her best move was punting me over to Kevin in the sports department when a position became available. On the same day Lisa retired, Kevin also moved on to a new professional adventure following a decorated twenty-eight-year run of leading one of the most accomplished sports sections in the country. I was pretty raw when I joined Kevin's staff, but he was patient with me and always provided positive feedback. He encouraged creative thinking and writing and pushed me to make sure my next story was better than the previous one. It was while working with Lisa and Kevin in Troy that I first wrote about and became intrigued with the remarkable life of John Morrissey. Thank you both for everything.

Thank you also to Stevie Edwards, the commissioning editor of this book, without whom this would still be a concept instead of a reality. I would also like to acknowledge the outstanding creative team at The History Press for delivering a polished final product.

Even though I have likely raised their blood pressure a tick or two on occasion, my parents, Tom Bouyea and Pam O'Brien Bouyea, have always believed in me as a writer and a son. I hope I have made them proud. Better and more loving parents have never existed. This one's for you.

To Julie Beth Franklin, thank you for your love, patience and understanding during the writing of this book. I look forward to a lifetime of incredible adventures with you. The best people in life make those around them better. I am fortunate and grateful to have several such people in my corner.

Finally, I would like to thank the incomparable John Morrissey, a character the likes of whom the best fiction writers would have difficulty imagining. I hope I did your story justice.

BRIEN BOUYEA
Saratoga Springs, New York
December 2015

HOPE AND DREAMS

John Morrissey brazenly represented the concept of what it meant to live the American dream during the nineteenth century. In a violent and uncompromising era defined by killers, thieves, thugs and political devils, Morrissey used his natural gifts—prodigious fists, a keen intellect and sheer ambition—to rise to heights his pedigree suggested were unattainable. With an unapologetic and unappeasable nature, he bucked the substantial odds against him as a poor Irish immigrant to better his lot in life and make a notable imprint on a period in which only bold men prospered.

Morrissey's life was and remains a fascinating study in contrasts. He was both merciless and compassionate. He experienced the hellish reality of extreme poverty and the spoils of great wealth. He was an illiterate gang member in his youth and revered as America's most famous sports figure during his twenties. He became a legendary gambler, feared political enforcer, successful businessman, pioneer and impresario in thoroughbred racing and, most surprisingly, a prominent and respected politician later in life. He spent time plotting with coldblooded murderers and time strategizing with society's upper crust. Many considered him a hero and an inspiration, while others saw only a bully concerned singularly with personal gain. Loved and feared, respected and detested, John Morrissey was the subject of polarizing judgments throughout society, kaleidoscopic opinions dependent on the vantage point from which they originated. By all accounts, it was an exciting and interesting existence that could not have been foreseen, one that produced a unique and complicated legacy.

BARE KNUCKLES & SARATOGA RACING

The journey began in Ireland, a country predominantly forsaken of hope when John Morrissey was born on February 12, 1831, in Templemore, County Tipperary. His parents, Timothy and Julia, lived a typical existence of the time, bound to the shackles of poverty with only a flicker of hope life could be anything more. Tim Morrissey was the personification of the clichéd Irishman. He enjoyed drinking and brawling and brought home paltry wages insufficient for supporting his wife and newborn child. His employment history featured a nondescript pattern of drifting from job to job as a common laborer, lacking any realistic prospects for financial security. These were among the darkest of times in Ireland's history, and stories such as Tim Morrissey's were rampant throughout the country. Ireland was overrun by the English, and the majority of the peasant natives had little more to eat than salted potatoes if they were fortunate and boiled weeds if they were not. In this age of the Protestant Ascendancy, it was hell to be an Irish Catholic. Famine became intertwined with disease, as the parasitic bacterial infection typhus killed an estimated 100,000 Irish from 1816 through 1849. The deck was stacked against people such as the Morrisseys.

Now entrusted with the care of their infant son, Tim and Julia Morrissey sought to escape the hardships and horrors of their homeland. Ireland tendered little hope for a poor family to make any progression toward improved economic or social standing, but America, they believed, offered that grand gift of opportunity. In America, a blank canvas awaited. Stories of the Irish crossing the Atlantic Ocean and realizing their dreams in New York City and elsewhere were common in Templemore. Even if they were more myth than reality, the outlook for a decent life in America was significantly greater than in Ireland. There was hope.

So Tim and Julia Morrissey scraped together what little money they could in the next year. In August 1832, they headed north to Belfast with baby John in tow and boarded an immigrant ship bound for America. Their funds were just enough to secure passage aboard a packed vessel that reeked of unwashed human flesh. Throughout the grueling, month-long voyage, several passengers became gravely ill and died of disease as the ship crawled across the Atlantic. The Morrisseys, however, were fortunate and survived the tumultuous ordeal in good order.

The miserable excursion came to a conclusion as the Morrisseys arrived safely in New York City in late September 1832. Hundreds of thousands of Irish immigrants were entrenched throughout the New York boroughs, but the Morrisseys chose not to linger in the city. They opted instead to make their way upstate to Troy, a developing industrial city and shipping port in

THE REMARKABLE LIFE OF JOHN MORRISSEY

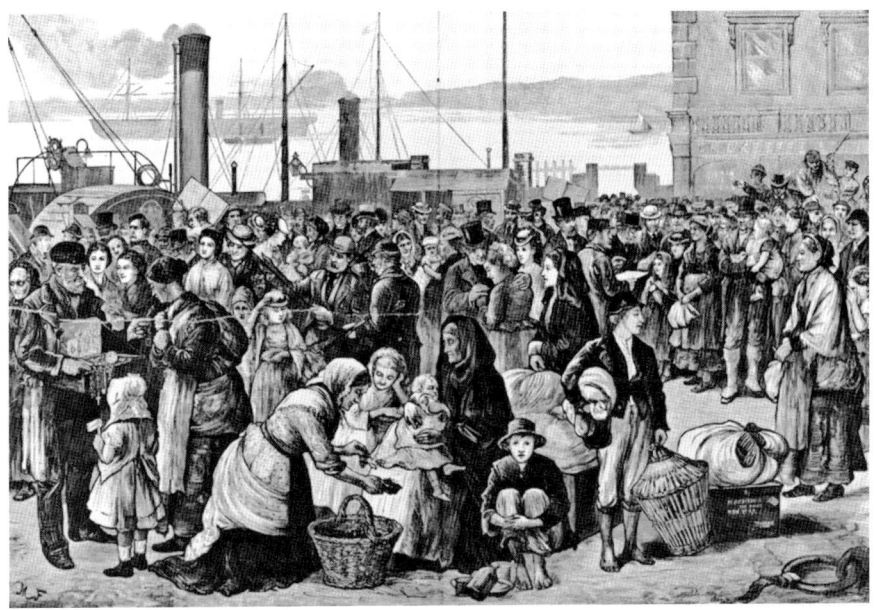

An immigration scene along the New York City docks from the nineteenth century. *From Harper's Weekly.*

Rensselaer County located 140 miles north of New York. Situated on the eastern bank of the Hudson River, Troy was a popular landing spot for immigrants seeking an alternative to New York City. The Morrisseys knew other families with Templemore roots who lived in Troy. The small sense of familiarity Troy provided was more alluring than the great unknown that greeted them upon their arrival in New York.

Ireland was now just a bad memory for the Morrisseys. The new beginning they so desperately coveted was before them in Troy. The city was nothing fancy or refined, but it did gain a measure of notoriety when quartermaster provisions for the War of 1812 were shipped from there. A local butcher and meatpacker named Samuel Wilson helped supply the army, and according to legend, barrels stamped "U.S." were interpreted by the troops to be from their "Uncle Sam," a personification of the United States. The mythic character of Uncle Sam and his patriotic pride has been associated with Troy ever since.

Troy was a logical spot for the Morrisseys to settle. It had yet to reach the pinnacle of its prosperity later achieved through the steel industry, but the city was on the upswing and bustling with activity. Troy served as a shipping transfer point for meat and vegetables from Vermont that were sent by the

Hudson River to New York City. The Federal Dam at Troy headed the tides on the Hudson, and steamboats plied the river on a regular basis. This trade was increased considerably after the construction of the Erie Canal, as its eastern terminus was located directly across the Hudson from Troy at Cohoes beginning in 1825.

For the Morrisseys, however, the great promise of Troy proved to be simply an illusion, and the city could only be considered a marginal upgrade from Templemore. Although humming with activity, Troy was in fact quite poor and drab, similar in many ways to Templemore. But for better or worse, this is where they would remain and cultivate their new life. Tim managed to secure work along the Hudson River docks as a jack-of-all-trades laborer. He had steady employment, but the compensation was minimal: a dollar and six drinks of whiskey a day. The Morrisseys scraped by, saved what little they could and eventually purchased a small house that was reminiscent of their rundown accommodations in Ireland.

As the years passed, Tim and Julia had seven more children in addition to John—all of them girls—and making ends meet became increasingly problematic with Tim's limited income. The Morrisseys were again living in extreme poverty, and their dreams of prosperity in America had faded away. They were in a new land, but the all-too-familiar hardships the Morrisseys faced in Templemore followed them to Troy. Nothing significant ever became of the Morrissey girls. Most of them married young, had children of their own and lived lives of poverty that were reflective of their upbringing and limited education. John Morrissey, however, followed a different path through life.

Although he received only one year of formal schooling before he was forced to join the workforce to help his family, John Morrissey was intelligent and driven. This was evidenced by the fact that he taught himself to read and write around the age of nineteen. Detesting his family's circumstances, young Morrissey used the dirt-poor existence that soured generations of his family as a motivator to make something significant of his life. Along with a sense of purpose, Morrissey acquired incredible physical strength and a hot temper, traits that would serve him well during his youth and beyond.

With his family in desperate need, John Morrissey took his first job at Orr's, a wallpaper factory in Troy. He worked sixty hours a week for the grand sum of two dollars. John detested the manual labor and quickly grew bitter with the dismal working conditions and miniscule compensation, but employment options were limited for poor Irish boys of his circumstance. After a year at Orr's, Morrissey moved to another position in the city at Burden Iron Mills.

THE REMARKABLE LIFE OF JOHN MORRISSEY

He was making better money now—five dollars per week—and the grueling physical labor aided in the development of his rugged physique. In 1846, at the age of fifteen, Morrissey gained employment with Johnson, Cox & Co., a stove company, where he was paid the decent sum of nine dollars a week. Morrissey was steadily climbing the labor ranks, but the money was never enough to make a difference for the family and the work never appealed to him.

Even with John's contributions, the Morrisseys were always teetering on the brink of destitution. For all the incessant labor of father and son, the family had nothing. It would always be that way. John's hostility toward his life and his family's place in the world began to grow. He started using his fists to settle disputes, as the action and violence appealed to his vicious and brooding persona. The men of Troy's mills and factories routinely settled their quarrels via brutality and bloodshed, an environment John Morrissey flourished in. His foes were older and bigger than he was in most instances, but John was freakishly strong, possessed uncommonly quick reflexes and could take a punch. He also had tremendous confidence in his fistic abilities. That swagger—or arrogance, as many perceived it—tended to rankle the fighting thugs throughout Troy, but there was little they could do about it. John Morrissey served up one beating after another, thrashing Troy's most accomplished brawlers. His fists were sledgehammers, and his jaw was as sturdy as the material he helped forge at Burden Iron Works. Grown men were living in fear of a young beast named John Morrissey.

At the age of sixteen, Morrissey became acquainted with a man named Alex Hamilton, one of the most disreputable figures in Troy. Hamilton owned a brothel that was despicable even by whorehouse standards. The men who frequented his establishment were the dregs of society whose only loves in life were booze, brawls and the prostitutes who occupied the upstairs rooms of sin. It was a lawless venue where bones were broken and blood was shed. Hamilton avoided the nuisance of law enforcement through handsome bribes, but the authorities finally insisted he keep a lower profile and curtail the daily violence or risk being shut down. John Morrissey was ideal for such a task.

Hamilton had a reputation for paying his bouncers well, but seldom did they last long. The pay was not worth the beatings they regularly suffered from the hardened factory workers and river pirates who were always seeking trouble. Hamilton needed an alternative solution. He had heard tales of Morrissey's exploits as a fighter, but he was a long way from being convinced that someone so young could handle the dangerous clientele that his brothel catered to. Still, Morrissey's reputation intrigued Hamilton, who sent an emissary to the young slugger. Morrissey showed up a couple days later to see if an offer would be forthcoming.

Upon first glance, Hamilton was impressed with what he saw in Morrissey. The boy was handsome and almost six feet tall with a chiseled frame. He projected an aura of confidence, and Hamilton noticed Morrissey could "move with the killing grace of a big cat," according to a contemporary account in the *Troy Times*. Hamilton knew Morrissey possessed an enthusiasm for fighting, and it was apparent that he featured the physical attributes required for such hazardous work. Morrissey was making a respectable wage at Johnson, Cox & Co., so Hamilton needed to extend a lucrative offer to obtain his services. Morrissey shocked Hamilton when he demanded the exorbitant compensation of twenty dollars per week. It was a sum Morrissey refused to negotiate. Hamilton had never paid more than twelve dollars a week for a bouncer, and he was irritated that Morrissey thought so highly of his worth.

Although taken by surprise that Morrissey had the audacity to ask for such a fee, Hamilton was willing to consider it—if Morrissey was as good as he said he was. If the strapping youngster could maintain order in the barroom and bedrooms, Hamilton would save a considerable sum in smashed glasses and mirrors alone. Perhaps it was a wise investment to make. But first, Hamilton needed some convincing that Morrissey could indeed vanquish the vile scum that brought his business such trouble. Morrissey knew he had to teach a lesson to one of Hamilton's most unruly patrons in order to prove his worth. He pointed out Bibber M'Geehan, an infamous dock rat from nearby Albany who was sitting at the end of the bar. M'Geehan was well known for his fighting exploits, and his methods were most cruel. He had gouged out the eyes of several opponents and even bit the nose off a man inside Hamilton's establishment.

"You want me to prove it? Bibber M'Geehan is at the bar," Morrissey said, according to an exchange documented in *Brandy for Heroes* by Jack Kofoed. "Will he do as a sample?"

"You couldn't pick a better," Hamilton responded.

Morrissey went to work. He confidently approached M'Geehan as the bearded bully was having a drink at the bar. M'Geehan stood six feet tall and packed two hundred muscular pounds onto his frame. Morrissey told M'Geehan to walk out and never come back. M'Geehan responded to Morrissey's directive with a hearty laugh, prompting John to deliver an immediate and decisive response. Morrissey unleashed a devastating right hand that struck M'Geehan's jaw. It was a tremendous shot that immediately

THE REMARKABLE LIFE OF JOHN MORRISSEY

closed M'Geehan's eyes. In an instant, M'Geehan's legs went limp, his head crashed into the bar's brass railing and his body tumbled to the floor. With one purposeful swing and hit, Morrissey announced his presence with authority and clobbered one of Hamilton's most malevolent regulars.

Wasting no time, Morrissey scooped up the unconscious M'Geehan, dragged him through the barroom and unceremoniously chucked him onto the street. Hamilton knew he had his man. No negotiation would be necessary. Morrissey had lived up to his advanced billing with his one-punch knockout of the troublemaker. He was a force to be reckoned with.

Hamilton's response: "Twenty it is!"

It didn't take long for Morrissey to effectively establish himself as Hamilton's muscle. John was categorical in the beatings he doled out to the house's unruly patrons. Morrissey leveled one goon after another, and the word quickly made the rounds that the young fighter was not to be trifled with. For Hamilton, it was money well spent, and his establishment quieted down significantly. For Morrissey, for the first time in his young life, he was starting to map out his future.

Although he had no remorse about pulverizing the troublemakers who haunted Hamilton's whorehouse, Morrissey was not a heartless menace. There are no incidents on record of him thrashing helpless victims or instigating a fight with an overmatched adversary. Still, brawling was a way of life in Troy, and Morrissey had seen men beaten to death in the mills and factories and along the docks. Violence was a part of the Irish culture and the Troy landscape. It was all Morrissey knew.

While he was earning good money in the employ of Hamilton, it would only be a matter of time before Morrissey grew tired of the tedious thumping of such men. He would not rise to great heights in such an environment. Morrissey dreamed much bigger. He dreamed of New York City and becoming a fixture on its grand stage. Getting there and establishing himself, however, presented a challenge, as most of the twenty dollars Morrissey brought home each week went to his struggling family. John was as broke as everyone around him, but there was a way out.

There were numerous cargo ships that lined the Hudson River docks in Troy and Albany that routinely traveled south to the ports of New York City. One of these vessels would provide John his ticket to the city. Morrissey became acquainted with Captain Levi Smith, master and commander of the steamship *City of Troy*. Smith took a liking to Morrissey and offered him a position as a deckhand. The pay wasn't much, but for Morrissey the arrangement was more about opportunity than money.

BARE KNUCKLES & SARATOGA RACING

Captain Smith presided over all matters relating to his ship with an iron fist. He was a disciplinarian by nature and demanded respect from his crew. Alex Hamilton, meanwhile, was in disbelief that Morrissey would walk away from twenty dollars a week to do menial labor on a boat. Hamilton offered Morrissey twenty-five dollars a week to stay, and then thirty, but Morrissey rejected the overtures. Hamilton's mighty enforcer was taking his game elsewhere. John Morrissey had made up his mind to work for Captain Smith aboard the *City of Troy*. New York City beckoned.

There was another reason Morrissey desired to work on the *City of Troy*. He had become enamored with the captain's daughter, the beautiful and intelligent Susie Smith. As an uneducated son of a common laborer, Morrissey had no business with a refined daughter of a steamboat captain, and his pursuit of her was unlikely to be successful. Susie Smith was educated at what is now the posh Emma Willard School in Troy; John Morrissey was educated in the streets.

Morrissey's duties aboard the *City of Troy* were far from glamorous, but sometimes Susie Smith would stop by and engage in conversation when John was swabbing the deck or polishing the brass railings. Morrissey was always respectful around Captain Smith's daughter, carefully choosing his words and always being conscious not to appear too eager in her presence. At the same time, John desired to prove to Susie that he would become something more than a common ruffian fighting the perpetual battle against poverty.

Although he was no longer working for Hamilton, trouble still managed to find John Morrissey. There was the occasional dock worker or drunken fool who wanted to test John and see if his reputation as an elite fighter was warranted or simply a myth. Morrissey continued to hammer foes as often as they presented themselves. He grew more fearless with each encounter and believed his fistic abilities would translate into lucrative opportunities in New York City.

As a seventeen-year-old, Morrissey became, in his own words, the "chief devil" of Troy's "Down Town" gang. Naturally, the "Down Town" gang clashed with the "Up Town" gang, led by John O'Rourke and John Mackey, both of whom were in their mid-twenties. O'Rourke was an accomplished fighter who had "whipped everyone in the surrounding country," according to the *New York Times*. Morrissey and O'Rourke eventually ran into each other at Lawrence's Saloon on River Street in Troy. Morrissey proceeded to thoroughly defeat his older rival, but that was only the beginning of the story. Eight of O'Rourke's henchmen, including Mackey, challenged Morrissey, who subsequently fought and defeated each man in succession. Morrissey became an instant legend in Troy and beyond thanks to the whippings he handed out to O'Rourke and his soldiers. One of his opponents spoke of Morrissey's fighting prowess in the *New York Daily Tribune*: "John never seemed to know when he was licked, and, just as you got tired of thumping him, he kind o' got his second wind, and then you might as well tackle the devil as to try to make any headway against him."

Susie Smith began to let her guard down around John. He was charming and persistent and had genuine affection for her. Now all he needed to do was convince Captain Smith that he was worthy. Morrissey did his best to make a favorable impression on the captain through his hard work, but he had to become more than a steamboat deckhand if he was ever going to get the old man's blessing to court his daughter. That time was not yet at hand.

Morrissey believed he had to find success in New York. He didn't yet have a definitive plan, but he figured his fists would pave whatever road he chose. Perhaps he was destined for glory as a bare-knuckle fighter. Professional boxing was illegal at the time, but the sport was growing in popularity, and big money and fame were involved at the top levels. If not in the ring, there would be prospects on the streets, as Morrissey could use his muscle to climb the ranks in one of the city's many politically affiliated gangs. Troy suddenly seemed like the minor leagues.

NEW YORK

In an effort to enhance his reputation as an elite fighter and make a name for himself, John Morrissey set out for New York City in July 1849. He was seeking out trouble—and he knew where to find it. A few months earlier, Morrissey's former employer, Alex Hamilton, had been in Manhattan and dropped by the Americus Club, located at 28 Park Row. Hamilton was on his way back to Troy following a trip to see the American championship fight between titleholder Tom Hyer and James Ambrose, who was more commonly known as Yankee Sullivan.

There was tremendous interest in the pugilistic encounter between Hyer and Sullivan. Hyer was recognized as American champion after defeating George "Country" McCloskey in 101 rounds at New York's Caldwell's Landing in 1841. Hyer was a famous man with famous bloodlines. His father, Jacob, was one of the earliest professional fighters in America—and a damn good one. Various accounts have Jacob Hyer winning—or, depending on the source, fighting to a draw—against the superb English slugger Tom Beasley in New York City during October 1816. Many historians consider the Hyer-Beasley match the first notable prizefight held on American soil.

Without a legitimate challenger to his throne, Tom Hyer did not fight in the formalized setting of the ring again following the contest with McCloskey until he met Sullivan at Pool Island on Maryland's Chesapeake Bay in February 1849. Sullivan, meanwhile, had racked up victories against some respected opponents, including Hammer Lane, Tom Secor, Vincent Hammond and Billy Bell. There was tremendous public clamor for a bout

BARE KNUCKLES & SARATOGA RACING

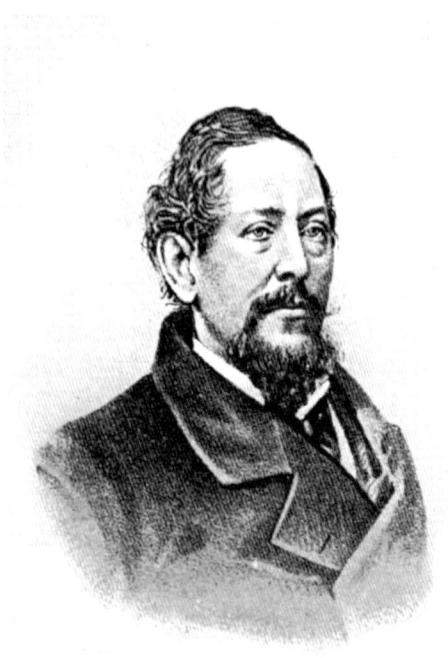

Tom Hyer, from a nineteenth-century tobacco card. *Courtesy of a private collection.*

pitting the champion Hyer against Sullivan. Eight years after he won the title, Hyer finally had a worthy challenger nipping at his heels.

Although considerable time had passed since he had been in an organized bout, Hyer, who was always fighting outside the ring, was considered a heavy favorite to defeat Sullivan, which he did with ease. The six-foot, two-inch Hyer weighed in around 220 pounds. He was considerably bigger and stronger than Sullivan, who stood five-foot-eight and weighed around 150 pounds. Hyer's raw power simply overwhelmed Sullivan. After seventeen minutes of one-sided fighting, Sullivan had been pulverized so thoroughly he could no longer continue.

Back in the Americus Club, Alex Hamilton sat at the bar as the conversation, as it routinely did, turned to the great pugilistic battles of the day. The establishment was presided over by Isaiah Rynders, a stalwart of the Native American Party, otherwise referred to as the Know-Nothings. Not to be confused with American Indians, the Native American Party was a street gang featuring some of the most feared fighters in New York City. Rynders wasn't much of a slugger himself, but he was regarded as a deadly combatant because of his skills with razorblades. He also owned a reputation as one of the top political enforcers of the era and could summon a motley crew of gangsters to do his bidding whenever he needed. At the time, Rynders and the Native Americans were an extension of the Whig Party, the opposition of Tammany Hall's powerful political machine. Rynders surrounded himself with some of the deadliest characters in New York, including William "Bill the Butcher" Poole, Tom Burns, "Dutch Charley"

THE REMARKABLE LIFE OF JOHN MORRISSEY

Duane, "One Eye" Daly and even the famous bare-knuckle champion Tom Hyer. New York's political leaders always needed street fighters to help implement their agendas, and many of the city's politicians enlisted Rynders and his collection of thugs for assistance in such matters. The work was both frequent and lucrative, making Rynders a powerful and wealthy man in New York.

Hearing the tales of the great New York street fighters, Hamilton couldn't resist the temptation to chime in and spread the gospel of Troy's mighty John Morrissey and his fistic exploits. Having personally witnessed the Hyer-Sullivan match, Hamilton remarked that he was not impressed with what he saw from the champion and said he was of the belief that Morrissey was superior. The ensuing events were reported on by Jack Kofoed in *Brandy for Heroes*.

"Ah, there's a lad," Hamilton said of Morrissey. "With all respect to you gentlemen, he is the greatest fighter in the world. Unless you have seen him yourself, you would scarcely credit it."

The comment drew the ire of "Dutch Charley" Duane, who issued a stern response to Hamilton.

"There ain't a man in the place that couldn't murder that farmer o' yours," Duane said. "Just send him down, and I will agree to bite off his ears."

Cognizant it would not be wise to further antagonize this dangerous collection of hoodlums, Hamilton did not extol the virtues of Morrissey's pugilistic abilities beyond his initial remark. As a conciliatory gesture, Hamilton bought the men a round of drinks and kept his opinions to himself the remainder of the night. Once he got back to Troy, however, Hamilton told Morrissey of his experience with Rynders and his men and how "Dutch Charley" Duane spoke of making the young fighter's ears keepsakes of a proper pasting.

"I've been wanting to go to New York for a long time," Morrissey said to Hamilton. "Now I've got a good excuse. I'll drop in on Dutch Charley and have a word with him."

"They are bad people," Hamilton responded.

"The worse the better," Morrissey said. "I'll go the next trip the *City* makes…and stop off this time, maybe for quite a spell."

This was the opportunity Morrissey was looking for. He could go to New York and take the city by storm. He could fight, make money and become a person of significance. Morrissey's frame had filled out. He stood six feet tall, weighed around 175 pounds and possessed elite strength, cat-like reflexes and an iron will that complemented his iron jaw.

BARE KNUCKLES & SARATOGA RACING

Morrissey had been to New York City before when the *City of Troy* traveled south along the Hudson, but this time he had a purpose and a career to start. Unaccompanied on this mission, Morrissey confidently made his way through the city and arrived at 28 Park Row. There was no turning back. The Americus Club was filled with its regulars, killers and thugs who featured bushy mustaches, scarred faces and classic black top hats. Young Morrissey, with his beardless face and patched trousers, must have looked like an alien when he entered the barroom.

This was an arena suitable only for battle-hardened brawlers willing to maim and kill at the drop of a hat. John Morrissey, still a teenager, was wandering into a potential slaughterhouse. As he pressed his way through the Americus Club, Morrissey noticed the filthy scowls of the bar's patrons fixated on him. These were men with bad intentions. Morrissey instantly surmised that they would not hesitate to do him harm. Still, he made his way toward the bar, showing no fear, as he knew any perceived weakness or uncertainty in his mannerisms could quickly lead to his dismemberment.

"Is Dutch Charley Duane here?" Morrissey asked the barkeep, who happened to be Rynders.

"No. Lady Suffolk is trotting today, and Charley went to see her," Rynders answered. "If it wasn't so damned hot all of us would have gone, too. Who are you?"

With his cold eyes fixated on the fresh-faced stranger, Bill Poole's mischievous voice entered the conversation.

"I'll bet it's the farmer from Troy," Poole shouted. "It can't be anybody but the farmer from Troy."

"Yes, I'm from Troy," Morrissey said. "And you…I don't know your name, mister…but you look like your mother would be a dollar street walker."

Poole was the most sinister of the men in the room. Bill the Butcher was a known killer who had made his mark by dicing up several foes with carving knives. He also had a history of gouging out eyeballs with his thumbs, and on occasion he would chew off the nose or feast on the chin of a hapless adversary. John Morrissey had just called out one of the most lethal individuals in all of New York, and he intended the insult to lead to a confrontation. He didn't know anything about Poole, but he planned to make an example of him. Morrissey stood only a few feet from Bill the Butcher as the tension in the barroom reached a crescendo. The fighter from Troy was ready to display the bone-crushing capabilities of his fists. The opportunity that Morrissey so desperately sought, however, did not materialize on this day.

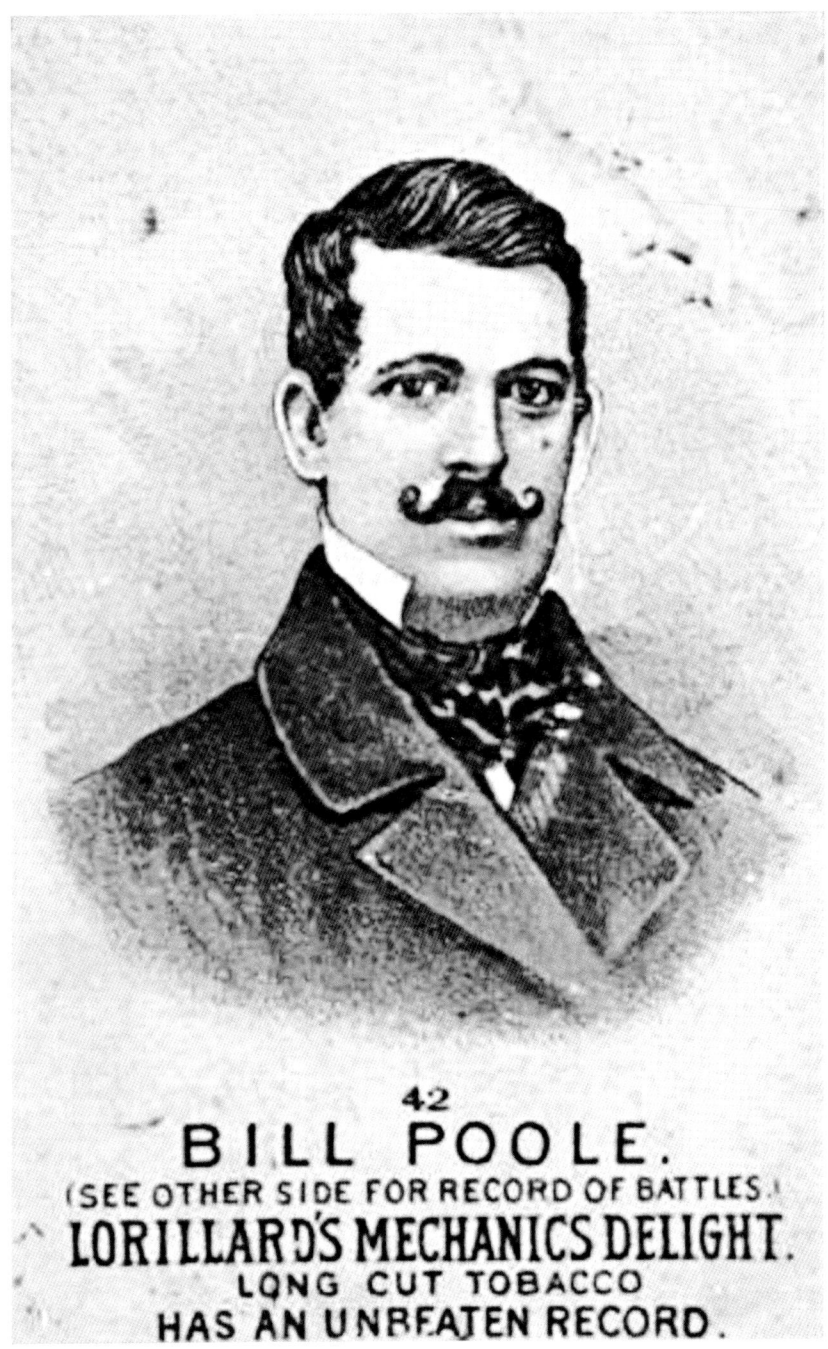

"Bill the Butcher" Poole, from a nineteenth-century tobacco card. *Courtesy of a private collection.*

As he prepared for battle with Poole, the unexpected happened. Instead of a showdown with one of New York's most notorious fighters, Morrissey suddenly found himself on the barroom floor with the shadow of death circling above. Morrissey had been struck in the back of the head with a brass spittoon and lost his footing. An angry mob quickly descended on the fallen fighter, and the welcoming party went in for the kill. A half dozen men began pummeling Morrissey with fists, boots, clubs and bottles. The Troy invader began gushing blood from numerous wounds, and the mob looked at him as a corpse for its pleasure.

Morrissey somehow managed to fight his way back to his feet. He had shown a remarkable threshold for absorbing pain, and many in the room could not comprehend how he was functional considering the damage inflicted upon him. Dazed and bloodied, Morrissey got in a few retaliatory blows before he was once again thumped in the back of his skull with a club. Face down on the floor, blood oozed from Morrissey's unconscious body. Bill Poole, "One Eye" Daly, Tom Burns and several others closed in, ready to end the affair.

"Let 'im alone...let 'im alone. You, Bill...you, 'One Eye'...get away, or by God, I'll use this knife on you!"

Morrissey's blood-thirsty assailants slowly backed away from the helpless figure beneath them. It was Isaiah Rynders, the proprietor of the Americus Club, who had unexpectedly come to Morrissey's aid. Wielding a double-edged blade, Rynders shielded Morrissey in a defensive pose, ready to uncoil and strike like a cobra if his call for mercy was not adhered to.

"We ought to kill him," Poole said.

"None o' you are goin' to do anything to that boy. Why, you fools, we need a fighter like him," Rynders said. "Did anybody ever stand up to you fellows the way he did? Things are goin' to be hot in this city, my buckos, and we can find a place for the farmer."

Rynders signaled for a couple of his bartenders to come forward.

"Carry him upstairs and call a doctor. Alex Hamilton was right," Rynders said. "There ain't a man in the world can fight like this youngster. I'll have plenty of use for him."

Rynders envisioned adding Morrissey to his impressive contingent of deadly enforcers to aid the Whigs in their power struggle with Tammany Hall. The Whigs and their street soldiers in the Know-Nothings gang detested the influx of immigrants into New York City. Morrissey, who hailed from a poor immigrant family, was exactly the sort of folk the Know-Nothings detested, but Rynders saw great potential in the youngster and figured he would be grateful for saving his life.

THE REMARKABLE LIFE OF JOHN MORRISSEY

While not in favor of the directive to halt their attack on Morrissey, Poole and the others respected Rynders's decision and decided to back off. Morrissey had been beaten to within an inch of his life, but he would live… he would recover…he would fight another day.

OLD SMOKE

There was little doubt John Morrissey would have met his demise on the floor of the Americus Club if not for the blade of Isaiah Rynders, who thought the young slugger from Troy would be a useful instrument as a street soldier in New York's contentious political battles. Rynders was not the sort of fellow who would have normally opposed to the likes of Morrissey being carved to a corpse, but he figured the boy would be grateful and pledge his allegiance for saving his life.

Following the gruesome beating, Morrissey spent several days and nights in a bed upstairs from the Americus Club barroom. Rynders called in a doctor to sew up the numerous gashes on Morrissey's face and attend to the various other wounds that covered his frame. Once Morrissey recovered, Rynders envisioned him helping the Know-Nothings in the city's election wars. The New York political scene was a scorching cauldron of corruption with the various parties of the day always in need of muscle on the street to manipulate voting results. Morrissey would be ideal as a "shoulder hitter," an intimidator who would literally drag immigrants to the polls and ensure they voted as instructed.

While grateful to Rynders for his intervention against Poole and his minions, Morrissey was not sold on the idea of shaking down immigrants. He had much in common with the bewildered dreamers who sought a new life in America, and the reality of this work hit close to home. Morrissey, however, also recognized that such a job could possibly lead to greater rewards if he proved proficient in the tasks assigned to him. Morrissey eventually agreed to work for Rynders, but he decided to head back to Troy for a bit before entering into the shoulder-hitting profession.

John Morrissey's face was a shocking sight upon his return to Troy. He was fortunate his eyes had not been clawed out, but his skull was covered with dried cuts, stitches and grotesque discoloring and swelling. Morrissey had only returned home to stay out of trouble while he recovered and to visit his family and Susie Smith. He cherished the time home, especially the opportunity to see Susie, but Morrissey was growing restless. The allure of New York was too powerful to resist. After a short stay in Troy, Morrissey returned to New York more determined than ever.

Morrissey eventually grew to like and trust Isaiah Rynders, but working for him was inevitably going to be an awkward fit because of Rynders's affiliation with the Native Americans. The Know-Nothings despised any individual not born in America, as well as those not of Protestant faith. Morrissey—Irish, Catholic and a poor immigrant—embodied everything the Native Americans abhorred. The economic realities of the United States were a major factor in the problems the immigrants faced and a key reason the Native Americans objected to their residency in America. Poole and his like-minded brethren believed there simply were not enough employment opportunities for all the foreigners who were arriving in droves. The immigrants were willing to work for less pay, and therefore those born on American soil would suffer as a result of it.

The Native American Party first formed as a secret society. There were strict rules and ideologies, as well as rugged initiations and solemn oaths. The pioneers of the organization were Protestants of British lineage who had been spreading anti-Catholic hatred throughout New York for years before John Morrissey arrived on the scene. These men were tagged as "Know-Nothings" because of the secretive nature of the organization. When asked about the group's activities by an outsider, a member of the Native American Party was instructed to say, "I know nothing."

Similar groups that preceded the Native American Party's rise to prominence in the 1840s were the driving force behind anti-Catholic riots in New York as early as 1806. A quarter century after those first anti-Catholic uprisings, Samuel Morse, the inventor of the telegraph, authored a book called *A Conspiracy Against the United States*. Morse's work was filled with wild accusations that the Roman Catholic Church was responsible for dangerous political activity in America. Morse insinuated that Catholic immigrants were plotting against the American government and were receiving direct orders from Rome that undermined the principles established by the

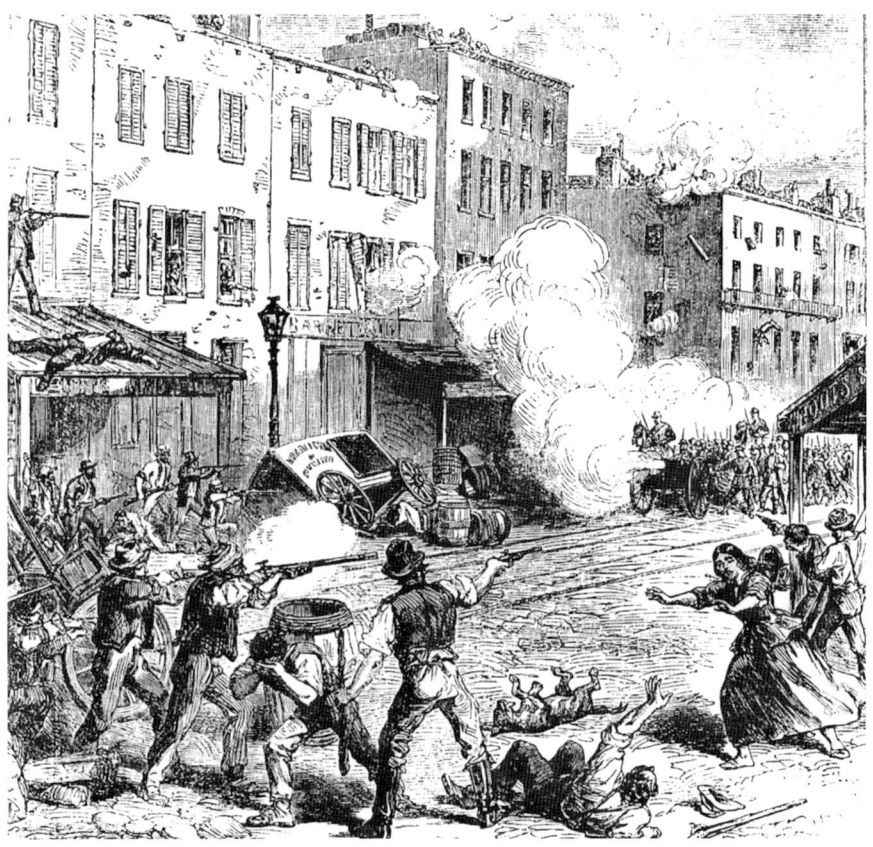

A depiction of the nineteenth-century violence in the Five Points in New York City. *Library of Congress.*

American Revolution. The book was a firestorm of hysteria that led to battle lines being drawn between Catholics and Protestants, as well as between immigrants and those born in America.

Riots were common in nineteenth-century New York. In 1835, a mob killed several Irishmen in the Five Points as a response to the forming of an Irish military regiment. The Native Americans did everything they could to suppress any movement by the Irish that could potentially lead to their rise in American society. The Irish, more than any other nationality, were regarded as the biggest threat to the Native Americans because of their sheer numbers, which were growing every day. There were significantly more Irishmen pouring into New York City during this time than any other nationality—and the natives despised each and every one of them.

Many of the immigrant groups began to take on military philosophies. The Know-Nothings and other native groups became increasingly nervous when they saw armed Irishmen taking part in military training in the streets. In response, native groups stockpiled their own weapons and formed rifle companies in hopes of thwarting potential immigrant rebellions. The Five Points, an infamous spot in Manhattan intersecting Centre Street to the west, the Bowery in the east, Canal Street in the north and Park Row in the south, was the stage for much of the bloody mayhem that was tearing the city apart.

The anti-Irish and anti-Catholic philosophies of the Native Americans began gaining political traction. By the early 1840s, there were other secret societies forming—the American Protestant Association, the Order of the Star Spangled Banner and the United American Mechanics, among several others—that followed the lead of the Native Americans. The members of these groups shared a common hatred for immigrants who desired to make a new life in the United States. They were also hypocrites. The Know-Nothings and the men in similar groups would never acknowledge that they were only a generation or two removed from ancestors of their own who arrived in America looking to build a better life. Now they were trying to deny others the same dream. So much for the land of opportunity.

In the 1840s, the Whig Party began an alliance with the Native Americans. The objective of the relationship for the Whigs was to gain influence and perhaps even seize control of some of the prominent Irish political wards. The Tammany leaders, meanwhile, focused much of their efforts on seeking the loyalty of New York's many Irish Catholics. They weren't concerned in the least bit about the plight of these poor folk, but they desperately desired their votes to maintain their political grip on the city. Corruption was everywhere. While the Whigs used the Know-Nothings as henchmen, Tammany Hall countered by affiliating with gangs such as the Dead Rabbits, a group mainly composed of hardened Irishmen who were growing in numbers and becoming just as violent as their counterparts.

The Dead Rabbits, Plug Uglies, Rip Raps and Wide Awakes were among the immigrant gangs of the era. They mostly began as security agents for street activists who were targets of the Native Americans when they sought to rally immigrants to work as a collective. However, the immigrant groups grew to be just as dangerous as the native ones. They gained a reputation for river piracy, looting of stores and acts of violence against police officers.

As war was being waged in the streets, the politicians were busy robbing the city treasury. Thousands of people in New York were starving or dying of disease. It was common to see girls who weren't yet teenagers working as prostitutes. Murder and mayhem were everywhere. This was the arena in which John Morrissey would begin a most interesting career.

The young Morrissey was indifferent to the economic, political, social and religious troubles that gripped New York in the late 1840s. He didn't have any attachment to the city, and its many issues were not at the forefront of his consciousness—at least not yet. Morrissey, however, clearly understood that to succeed in this environment he had to lead with his fists and be resolute in his actions. It was most unusual for a poor Irish immigrant such as Morrissey to be working as an immigrant runner for the Native Americans, but Rynders cared only about the muscle and votes he could provide. Morrissey was not their kind of people, but thanks to Rynders, he would get a pass and enter New York's gangland scene as a low-level thug in the employ of the Know-Nothings.

Numerous unsavory characters lurked along the docks of New York. They made a living by victimizing foreigners who were hoping to find a shot at prosperity in America. Most of these immigrants were easy fodder for the shoulder hitters, as many did not speak the language or understand the customs. Almost as soon as they got off the boats that carried them thousands of miles across the Atlantic Ocean, these weary souls were pounced upon to become pawns in the political wars. The foreigners were quickly naturalized by judges and provided citizenship documents so they could be eligible to vote in upcoming elections.

The shoulder hitters herded the immigrants like cattle. The various political parties and their immigrant runners constantly engaged in illicit activity. They were known to rob immigrants of whatever they had and then shuttle them off to boardinghouses, brothels and taverns to corrupt and indebt them. The proprietors of these establishments would pay the runners fees for sending the foreigners their way. Morrissey didn't have a taste for the work, but it put money in his pocket and he was proving to be a capable enforcer just as Rynders had envisioned. Morrissey's aggressiveness and ability to intimidate led him to become one of the top runners. He was earning a reputation for himself as someone who could produce results. However, the business of immigrant running was cutthroat, and Morrissey was making enemies in some circles as quickly as he was gaining respect in others.

Morrissey's success as a shoulder hitter drew the attention of Tom McCann, reputed to be among the top immigrant runners. McCann had become a wealthy man through his participation in this brutal line of work and didn't appreciate the fact that John Morrissey was invading his territory. McCann had long been an ace of his profession. This veteran menace of

BARE KNUCKLES & SARATOGA RACING

New York's underworld was of the opinion that this Morrissey kid from Troy needed to be removed from the equation. Morrissey, naturally, had other ideas. He planned to antagonize the notorious McCann and make an example of him. Tom McCann was to be a steppingstone for John Morrissey.

McCann traveled in the same circles as notorious New York underworld thugs such as Bill Poole and Tom Hyer. Although of Irish descent, McCann was born in America and therefore accepted by the Know-Nothings. The forty-year-old McCann was a barrel-chested savage who was every bit the physical equal of Morrissey, though an inch or two shorter. Although he had yet to come face to face with Morrissey, McCann let it be known throughout the city that he meant to do bodily harm to the youngster when the opportunity presented itself.

Morrissey was well aware of McCann's status among the shoulder hitters and had heard several tales of his physical prowess. Morrissey knew that if he were to defeat McCann in a rough-and-tumble street fight his status in New York would soar. Street credibility meant everything to Morrissey. So what would be the best way to embarrass and infuriate McCann and draw him out? By stealing his woman, of course.

Tom McCann was known as much for the woman he kept as he was for his status among New York's immigrant runners. McCann was intimate with the sultry Kate Ridgely, who was known throughout the city for her beauty and the illegal business she ran. Ridgely, in her mid-twenties, was the proprietor of New York's most infamous bordello. Her establishment was nothing like the filthy whorehouse owned by Alex Hamilton back in Troy where Morrissey used to deal with the drunken dregs of society. The women in Ridgely's establishment wore only the finest clothing and jewelry, and access to them was carefully vetted. Ridgely's business did not cater to the common folk of New York. Her clientele was required to have the deepest of pockets.

Ridgely offered the finest wines and the softest beds in New York, but the biggest attraction inside the brothel was Kate herself. It was said there was no other madam in the city who could match her beauty and intellect. Tom McCann was envied by many men because of it. Things were good for McCann. He was one of the most feared men in New York, thrived in a lucrative profession and had one of the city's most coveted women on his arm. He would be quite the conquest for John Morrissey.

Kate Ridgely was supposed to be off limits to the men in her bordello, but that didn't stop John Morrissey from making his move. He simply walked in one night looking for the desirable madam. The place was an eye-opener for Morrissey. The parlor was a grand room that was as lavishly furnished as any private home in the city. The only whorehouse Morrissey knew was Hamilton's dump in Troy. Instead of worrying about slugging it out with river thugs or cleaning up blood and broken glass, Morrissey was treated to champagne and offered his choice of the house's many beautiful women. Morrissey, however, was only interested in Kate Ridgely. He knew he was entering dangerous territory, but that was precisely the idea. Morrissey had never encountered a woman who combined beauty and sophistication the way Kate Ridgely did. He had fallen for the lovely Susie Smith back in Troy, but she was an innocent country lass in comparison. For Morrissey, Kate Ridgely would be an interesting adventure and a pawn in his plot to take down Tom McCann. She was impressed with Morrissey and allowed him into her bed.

John Morrissey became a regular in Kate Ridgely's bedroom, and tales of their hot affair quickly spread. Word would soon reach Tom McCann, prompting him to seek his vengeance. At least that's what Morrissey assumed and was counting on. Morrissey, of course, was quite boastful about his conquest of the supposedly unattainable Kate Ridgely. He remained conspicuous as he awaited the day he would be confronted by McCann, but weeks passed and their paths never crossed. Morrissey became frustrated. He wanted a showdown with McCann so he could build his reputation and graduate to more prosperous work.

Tom McCann had seemingly dropped off the face of the earth. Was he ducking Morrissey? Did he not care about the brash youngster bedding the woman who was supposed to be his? While Morrissey was going about his regular business on the docks, McCann was nowhere to be found. Morrissey inquired about the whereabouts of his target and continued to smear McCann's name in the streets in the hope it would draw him out into the open and into a fistic encounter.

Morrissey began to assume he had scared McCann into hiding. Having no more use for her, he moved on from Kate Ridgely. His objective was to use Ridgely to get to McCann, and she had served that purpose as best she could. Instead of occupying his time in the arms of the infamous madam, Morrissey was determined to canvass the underbelly of New York in search of the elusive McCann.

Word finally reached Morrissey in December 1849 that McCann had become a regular in the barroom and underground shooting gallery at the St. James Hotel on Broadway. Perhaps this was a trap. Perhaps McCann and several of his henchmen were setting Morrissey up for a gang assault similar to the one he barely survived the year before in the Americus Club. Morrissey wasn't about to make the same mistake twice. Instead of charging into the St. James in a blind rage, Morrissey exercised patience. He waited a couple days and scouted the location to make sure the environment would be favorable when he decided to enter. A light snow was falling on the city's cobblestone streets when Morrissey quietly slipped into the St. James on a cold winter's evening.

The St. James Hotel was a haven for the sporting men of New York. The place featured a popular shooting gallery in its basement, and the hotel bar was typically packed with some of the city's most unsavory characters. To Morrissey's disappointment, the lobby clerk told him McCann had not been in all day. Morrissey chose to stick around for a while just in case McCann made an appearance. He proceeded downstairs into the shooting gallery. The pungent aroma of pistol smoke filled the air as Morrissey entered the hotel basement. Warmth on this chilly night was courtesy of a pot-bellied stove in the center of the room. To pass some time, Morrissey decided to fire a few shots at the ducks in the gallery. He was at ease as he waited. A couple hours later, Tom McCann arrived on the scene. He greeted some acquaintances and was said to be in a jovial mood, but the cheerful tone in the room, according to an account in the *Police Gazette*, quickly vanished once Morrissey's voice bellowed over the clapping pistols.

"Men, if somebody took most of your business away, and finished by stealin' your girl, what would you do?"

McCann, aware of his adversary's ability with his fists, did not immediately respond. A tense silence overtook the room as the guns quieted. The only sound in the room was Morrissey's thundering voice.

"I did those things to Tom McCann," Morrissey continued. "I understand he's been around tellin' everybody what he was goin' to do to me."

Morrissey removed his coat and threw it on the counter. His words were measured, and he had the look of a wild animal in his eyes.

"Well, here I am…waiting. What do you think he'll do?"

McCann started to remove his own coat and moved cautiously toward Morrissey. John was as calm as could be and even cracked a sly smile at his enemy. After a few uncomfortable seconds, Morrissey cocked his right hand and unleashed a haymaker that struck McCann squarely in the mouth. Blood immediately began to flow from McCann's lips. The veteran brawler had been rocked. McCann lunged forward to engage Morrissey in a clinch. Once in close quarters, McCann attempted to extract Morrissey's eyes with his thumbs, but John was a heady fighter who was prepared for McCann's tactics. He quickly tucked his head into McCann's shoulder to avoid being gouged.

Morrissey began to wear McCann down by connecting with numerous powerful blows to the body and head, including an uppercut to McCann's chin that sent him reeling to the floor. It appeared that Morrissey was about to finish the job when McCann dove forward and wrapped his arms around Morrissey's waist. Both fighters lost their footing and tumbled toward the center of the gallery. The off-balance brawlers crashed into the stove, spilling a pile of scorching cherry-red coals across the floor. Both fighters were unable to regain their balance, and Morrissey fell to the floor under McCann, who pounced on his young adversary and pressed Morrissey's back into the burning coals.

The awful smell of cooked flesh began to fill the room. Morrissey writhed in excruciating pain. Suddenly, his near-death experience on the barroom floor of the Americus Club didn't seem so bad. McCann gripped Morrissey's throat and continued to hold him atop the sizzling coals as they dug deeper into his back. Sandy Lawrence, the manager of the pistol gallery, poured a bucket of water over McCann and the burning Morrissey. As a cloud of steam rose from the extinguished coals, Morrissey thrust himself upward and threw McCann across the room. Morrissey went into a demonic rage, closed on his enemy and began to hammer his skull with a ferocious series of crushing blows.

Morrissey knocked several of McCann's teeth down his throat while others scattered across the floor. Morrissey was unyielding as he continued his assault. He shattered McCann's nose and then unhinged his jaw. Morrissey would have likely beaten McCann to death if his adrenaline hadn't finally been overcome by the pain of the gruesome burns that covered his back. McCann's face was a frightful sight, and he was almost unrecognizable. His head had been carved into a bloody pulp by Morrissey's slashing punches. McCann remained unconscious until he was eventually dragged into the street and into a carriage that took him to a nearby hospital. McCann's days as New York's top immigrant runner were over. He was scarcely to be heard from again as his name faded into obscurity.

With his foe vanquished, John Morrissey wobbled over to the counter to retrieve his coat. He was clenching his teeth and grimacing but refused to cry out in pain. His pride would not allow such an admission of weakness. The shirt on Morrissey's back had been shredded from the blistering coals, revealing horrible burns that would scar him for life. Nobody would question the valor of John Morrissey ever again.

From that night forward, Morrissey was forever known as "Old Smoke." The moniker was a glorious testament to his remarkable courage and tolerance for pain. He was now the talk of the town. In the aftermath of his fiery destruction of Tom McCann, Morrissey immediately became both feared and revered throughout New York.

The influential New York politicians began to take notice of Morrissey's activities and successes. They valued him because he was a man of action and capable of getting results. He had successfully ascended to the top of the ranks among the shoulder hitters and vanquished a top rival in the field. He never took a liking to immigrant running, but it was a rung on the ladder he had to climb. Eventually, Morrissey's conscience got the best of him. Although it was profitable, and he was quite good at it, Old Smoke began to view his work as both cruel and petty. He knew he had to be a hard man to thrive in hard times, but intimidating and taking advantage of immigrants was not an honorable path in life and he would do it no more.

CALIFORNIA ADVENTURES

Word of John Morrissey's thrashing of Tom McCann quickly became the stuff of legend throughout New York City. In barrooms, along the docks and among the sporting gentry, Old Smoke's victory was the talk of the town. Although only nineteen years old, Morrissey was now among the most-known and feared fighters around. However, in the grand scheme of things, the victory did little to further Morrissey's ambitions. He had earned a reputation as a terrific and courageous fighter, but now what? Since he continued to send money home to his family, Morrissey had little to show for all his efforts as a shoulder hitter. The nature of the business was wearing on him, and he had no definitive plan of what to do next.

New York was filled with gambling houses. By some accounts, the city had more than four thousand of them in the mid-nineteenth century. Most of the gamblers who frequented these establishments were cheats, and the majority of the houses were generally regarded to be unscrupulous in their methods of bilking their players. Honest gamblers and fair parlors were hard to find. Knowing there was money to be made for daring men, it had all the makings of a perfect fit for John Morrissey.

The trade of immigrant running brought Morrissey some notoriety, but his growing disgust for the business and recognition that it would only take him so far convinced him it was time to walk away. So he did. While scouring the city for opportunities, Morrissey met a man named John Petrie, owner of a small gaming house on Church Street. It was a modest establishment located behind a hospital and was considered one of the few honest gambling venues in New York. There was no pretentiousness to it, and Petrie did a solid amount of business.

Petrie knew of Morrissey's fistic exploits and was impressed with his determination to make something of his life. He thought Old Smoke would make a fine assistant, and he promptly hired him upon learning he was out of the immigrant game. Morrissey learned much during his apprenticeship with Petrie. He studied and became skilled in games such as faro, poker, monte and dice. Morrissey also took special note of Petrie's business practices. Petrie ran an honest establishment because he believed it paid better in the long run and involved less risk. The percentage is always with the house, Petrie believed, so why develop a bad reputation or risk having a player pull a pistol on you? Old Smoke held his mentor in high regard and never forgot his philosophies.

While Morrissey was learning the ropes in the gambling trade, Captain Levi Smith, his old boss on the *City of Troy*, was planning on moving his family to New York City from Troy. Smith was a successful skipper and saw an opportunity to further enhance his shipping business by making New York the base of his operation. The Smiths settled on Hudson Street in Manhattan, and Morrissey continued to show interest in the captain's daughter, Susie.

Captain Smith was always wary of Morrissey. He did not dislike John, but he was appalled by his behavior and reputation in New York. The captain had heard all the stories of Old Smoke's immigrant running and knew of his terrible brawl with Tom McCann. Captain Smith didn't want his daughter to have any part in Morrissey's antics. John would have to continue to bide his time and hold off any thoughts of pursuing Susie Smith.

Old Smoke was becoming impatient in New York. He had learned a great deal from John Petrie, but he was still a subordinate in the Church Street gambling house and would only go so far there. Perhaps it was time for a fresh start elsewhere. Maybe…California!

Stories of the gold rush on the West Coast were told in every saloon in New York. The Astor House, specifically, was filled with sailors, shipbuilders and thrill-seekers who spoke of the riches available in California and exciting tales of the Forty-Niners. Morrissey desperately wanted a share of the riches and glory and began plotting his journey. Getting there, however, would not be easy.

For those with the means, a trip to California could be made by clipper ship. For those who could not afford the passage, the other option was a cross-country trek over the Old Spanish Trail. This took much longer and was extremely dangerous. This path led through the Mojave Desert and

THE REMARKABLE LIFE OF JOHN MORRISSEY

Death Valley, and many people who chose this route did not live to share their experience. Thousands set out from New York and New England in covered wagons seeking California riches and were never heard from again. Many died of illness or starvation or were murdered by Indian marauders. Morrissey had no interest in this game of roulette, but he did not have the funds to travel via clipper ship.

John Petrie was willing to help. Morrissey and another of Petrie's employees, Daniel "Dad" Cunningham, borrowed just enough money from Petrie to make their way to Panama. The adventurers arrived there in the autumn of 1850 and then stowed away on a cargo ship bound for San Francisco. Morrissey and Cunningham were discovered when Old Smoke intervened in a dispute aboard the ship. Morrissey saw a well-heeled man strike a young crew member and decided to get involved. The ship's captain appeared and demanded to see their tickets. Unable to produce any, the captain was about to put Old Smoke and Cunningham in irons when a commotion on the boat allowed them to slip away into the bowels of the vessel. Morrissey and Cunningham remained undiscovered for three days until the captain and his officers finally caught up with them.

Finally cornered, Morrissey and Cunningham were in big trouble. The captain considered throwing the stowaways overboard or dumping them in Acapulco, which was about fifteen hundred miles from San Francisco. Morrissey and Cunningham, however, caught a break. Fortune smiled upon them as a group of thugs began to organize a mutiny on the ship shortly after the stowaways were discovered. Needing more muscle to maintain control of the ship, the captain offered Morrissey and Cunningham safe passage to San Francisco if they would stand against the uprising. They quickly agreed and were armed by the captain with revolvers.

With the intimidating Morrissey and his companion Cunningham carrying weapons and in support of the captain and his crew, the mutineers backed down. The remainder of the journey was without incident. Morrissey and Cunningham were well fed and given suitable quarters. They finally arrived in San Francisco in January 1851. The town was dreary, and steady winter rains added to the somber tone. The streets of San Francisco were lined with wooden planks that covered the thick mud beneath. It was not a picturesque environment, but adventure and excitement were everywhere. Sailors, miners, mercenaries, fighters and gamblers flooded the streets and saloons. They were decked out in sombreros, velvet cloaks, serapes, red shirts and fancy boots with spurs. It was a different scene than New York, but the schemes were similar.

BARE KNUCKLES & SARATOGA RACING

San Francisco was filled with bars, gambling houses and theaters. There were bullfights and prizefights. The town was seemingly made for Old Smoke and his talents. Morrissey and Cunningham figured they would gather all the gold they could load up and return to New York as rich men, but they were too late. By the time Morrissey arrived in San Francisco, most of the gold in the area had already been staked, and thousands of miners had moved on to try their luck in Sacramento. Once again, Old Smoke had to improvise. His alternative to striking it rich in gold was found on the gaming tables. Morrissey and Cunningham knew what they were doing. They began to find success and steadily built their bankrolls. Their time under John Petrie's wing was paying handsome dividends.

Although he was making some money, Morrissey was growing bored with San Francisco. Old Smoke was a man of action, and he wanted to fight. It seemed the stars were aligning for Morrissey when word began to spread throughout town that Tom Hyer had arrived in California. Hyer had not fought in the ring since defeating Yankee Sullivan two years earlier, but he was still regarded as the American champion and highly respected as a pugilist. John Morrissey wanted a shot at the title. Hyer, however, had little interest in a fight with Old Smoke. Hyer hadn't trained in some time and was more interested in booze and women than the ring. Like Morrissey, he ventured to California seeking gold.

Hyer was accompanied in San Francisco by his trainer, the Englishman George Thompson, a savvy fighter in his own right and one of the most scientific boxers of the time. Morrissey made numerous challenges to Hyer, but the champion continued to refuse. Old Smoke was in tremendous physical condition, and at thirty-three years old, Hyer was no longer the fierce fighter he was only a couple years prior. Tired of Morrissey's badgering and unable to secure any gold, Hyer departed San Francisco and returned to New York.

Old Smoke couldn't get the champion to do battle so he sought a consolation prize—his trainer. While Hyer didn't stick around California, Thompson decided to stay and had no reservations about stepping in the ring. Thompson earned an easy victory over a fighter named Corwin Willis in July 1852 and then agreed to take on Morrissey. The bout was scheduled for August 31, 1852, at Mare Island, off the California coastline. Thompson was a seasoned veteran of the ring, but Old Smoke was by far the greater physical specimen.

Morrissey was disappointed that Hyer would not put his championship on the line, but a victory against Thompson would still be a tremendous feather in his cap. After all, there was good money at stake—$2,000 a side was put

THE REMARKABLE LIFE OF JOHN MORRISSEY

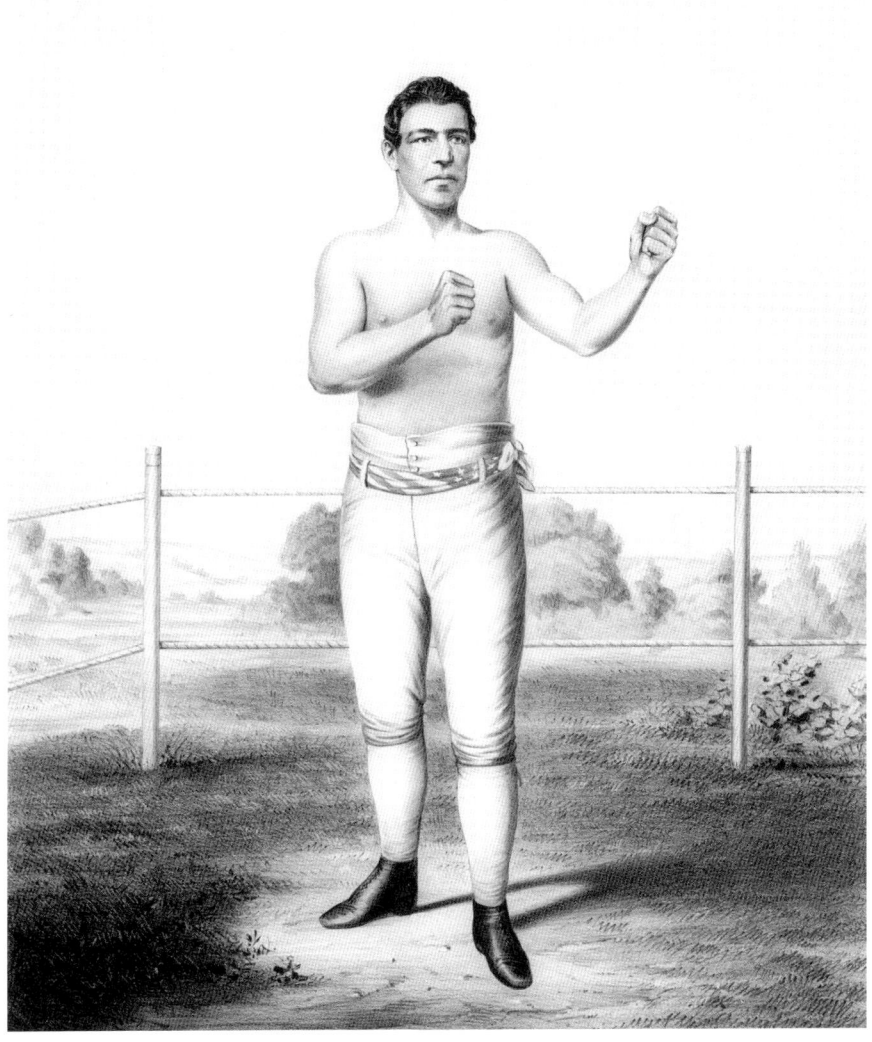

John Morrissey, portrayed by Currier and Ives, during his time as a bare-knuckle boxer. *Library of Congress.*

up—and Morrissey could return to New York with his head held high if he whipped Hyer's trainer after the champ wanted no part of the young Irishman. It would also be a small measure of revenge against the Americus Club gangsters. Tales of the frightening Know-Nothings, especially Bill the Butcher, reached all the way to California. Morrissey detested the celebrity

Poole and Hyer enjoyed and looked forward to whipping a man they regarded as a friend and associate.

The fight between Morrissey and Thompson was the biggest story of the California summer. Every tavern, bordello and gambling house was abuzz with debate of how the two combatants matched up. Would Thompson be able to use his scientific approach to befuddle and exasperate the inexperienced Morrissey? Could Old Smoke simply overwhelm Thompson with brute force? These points were endlessly argued in the days and nights leading up to the showdown.

The sun was cooking the morning of August 31, 1852, when a group of boats made their way to tiny Mare Island, located just outside of Vallejo, California. Morrissey and his backers boarded the steamship *Red Jacket*, while Thompson and his supporters arrived via the *West Point*. More than two thousand men arrived on various other ships at Mare Island. The strip of land was only a mile wide, but it was an ideal venue because there was no law enforcement with any jurisdiction to prevent the fight.

Both Morrissey and Thompson were in top condition for the fight. Although he neglected to study the rules of the London Prize Ring, Old Smoke made sure he was in peak physical form. Thompson likewise paid great attention to his training and appeared quick and agile.

The ring was surrounded by gamblers brandishing pistols, bearded miners and even some curious pirates. It was a wild and unpredictable environment, and wagers were made with sacks of gold. The crowd began to part as the two warriors made their way to the ring. The majority of the spectators aligned themselves with Morrissey, as Englishmen were generally not looked upon kindly. Old Smoke entered the ring with a wide smile and an air of confidence.

Morrissey, however, was quite naïve when it came to the rules of the ring. He wasn't versed in the significant differences between street brawling and the more formal pugilistic regulations of the London Prize Ring. The London Rules were originally drafted by England's Jack Broughton in 1743 and revised in 1838. Under the rules of the London Prize Ring, fighters could grapple with each other and throw their opponent to the ground. The sport was as much wrestling as it was boxing. Fighters were even allowed to wear spiked shoes. Rounds had no time limit and ended when a man was floored by a punch or throw. Fighters could also end a round and evade danger by dropping to the ground. Between rounds, the combatants were given thirty seconds to rest and eight additional seconds to "come to scratch," a return to the middle of the ring where a "scratch line" was drawn to square off with his opponent. There were no round limits. Fights went on until a man was unable to continue. While matches could have an enormous number of rounds, those rounds were often quick as fighters commonly would go down from minor blows to take advantage of the thirty-second rest period and escape more serious damage.

George Thompson knew all the ins and outs of the London Rules, while Morrissey was a novice. As the two fighters came to scratch, Thompson struck a conventional pose. In contrast, Old Smoke ignored all formality and charged toward his opponent with reckless abandon. Thompson simply sidestepped the rampaging Morrissey and then connected with a series of sharp blows that dazed Old Smoke. It quickly became evident Thompson could proficiently counter Morrissey's muscle with his slick skills.

Old Smoke steadied himself, but he hadn't learned his lesson yet. He again rushed wildly at Thompson, but the result was the same. The Englishman dodged Morrissey and responded with more quick shots to the skull. Old Smoke looked unprepared and overmatched in this formal environment. After being peppered for a few minutes, Morrissey wisely decided it was time to change tactics. Instead of charging like a bull, Old Smoke began to methodically stalk the veteran Thompson and eventually cornered him. Morrissey was then able to unleash a wrecking ball of a right hand that shook the Englishman. Old Smoke quickly followed by clinching his opponent and chucking him across the ring and onto the ground. The crowd roared with approval.

Thompson continued to fight cautiously in an effort to negate Morrissey's considerable strength advantage. The Englishman would wisely slip to the ground every time Old Smoke gained an advantage. Although his tactics were perfectly legal, Thompson drew the ire of the crowd for his unwillingness to slug it out with Morrissey. The mob came to see a war, not an exhibition of the finer points of the London Rules. Those in attendance generally viewed Thompson's methods as cowardly.

Thompson was able to hit Morrissey with tremendous accuracy throughout the bout. The blows, however, seemed to do little to deter Old Smoke. Morrissey displayed tremendous bottom and shrugged off the majority of Thompson's punches. Now it was the Englishman who was growing frustrated. Thompson threw everything he had at Morrissey and still the young slugger pressed on.

As the rounds progressed, Old Smoke grew stronger and Thompson began to wear down. Morrissey almost ended the battle in the tenth round. He smashed both sides of Thompson's face with a rousing left-right combination. Thompson crumpled to his knees in excruciating pain as the crowd erupted in applause. Morrissey sensed that Thompson's spirit had been dulled and that the end was near.

Thompson somehow managed to make it to scratch for the eleventh round, but it was evident he didn't want anything more to do with Old Smoke, who was gaining momentum and steadily sapping the vitality of his adversary. As the eleventh round commenced, Morrissey wasted no time in seeking a quick resolution to the affair. He immediately cracked Thompson on the jaw with a heavy right hand that appeared to do the trick. Thompson lost his balance and fell toward Old Smoke. As he began to go down, Thompson grabbed Morrissey by the hip of his drawers in desperation and slung him to the ground. Both men fell hard.

Old Smoke was incensed at Thompson's tactics. The referee immediately disqualified Thompson for the blatant foul, and Morrissey was declared the victor. The bout didn't end with the decisive knockout Old Smoke desired, but it was still a win. Thompson slithered from the ring as Morrissey's backers fêted their hero. Old Smoke became the toast of California. He had defeated a respected fighter and in the process proved that his toughness and tenacity could overcome a lack of scientific expertise in the ring. Word of Morrissey's triumph traveled all the way back to New York. It was not a popular tale inside the Americus Club.

Morrissey pocketed $2,000 of purse money and collected an additional $1,000 from a side bet for defeating Thompson. Along with his winnings on the gambling tables, Old Smoke had acquired a nice bankroll. Morrissey could have stayed in California and built on his success there, but New York had greater appeal to him. Returning east, Morrissey hoped his success in the ring would allow him to climb a rung or two on the political ladder. Maybe now Tom Hyer would agree to a fight. For certain, Old Smoke's days of being a shoulder hitter along the docks were a thing of the past. John Morrissey was now a known man on both coasts. His star was on the rise.

THE AMERICAN CHAMPION

John Morrissey returned to New York from California in the fall of 1852 with an enhanced fighting reputation and some money. He was only twenty-one years old, but there was plenty of buzz that Morrissey was as good as any fighter in the land. It was widely speculated it would only be a matter of time until he became champion of America. Tom Hyer would eventually have to fight him or relinquish the title.

While he waited for his shot at fistic immortality, Old Smoke became more engaged in New York's seedy political arena. Morrissey had plenty of notoriety now and had graduated from shoulder hitting. The city's movers and shakers began to seek him out for important tasks they didn't want to dirty their hands with. One of the individuals who held Old Smoke in high regard was Fernando Wood, who had aspirations of becoming the city's mayor.

Wood was born in Philadelphia in 1812 and arrived in New York in 1836. He opened a saloon and a grocery store and financially prospered in the city, becoming a millionaire by the age of twenty-eight. Like many men of the era, Wood didn't have any scruples, but he was cunning and driven to succeed. He built his wealth through rigged lotteries in partnership with his brother, Benjamin, who later became publisher of the *New York Daily News*. Fernando Wood also made considerable money in the shipping business and through shady real estate deals. The Wood brothers were known as flat-out thieves—and nobody seemed to care. In 1840, Fernando Wood was elected to the U.S. House of Representatives from New York's Third District and served until 1843. Following his term

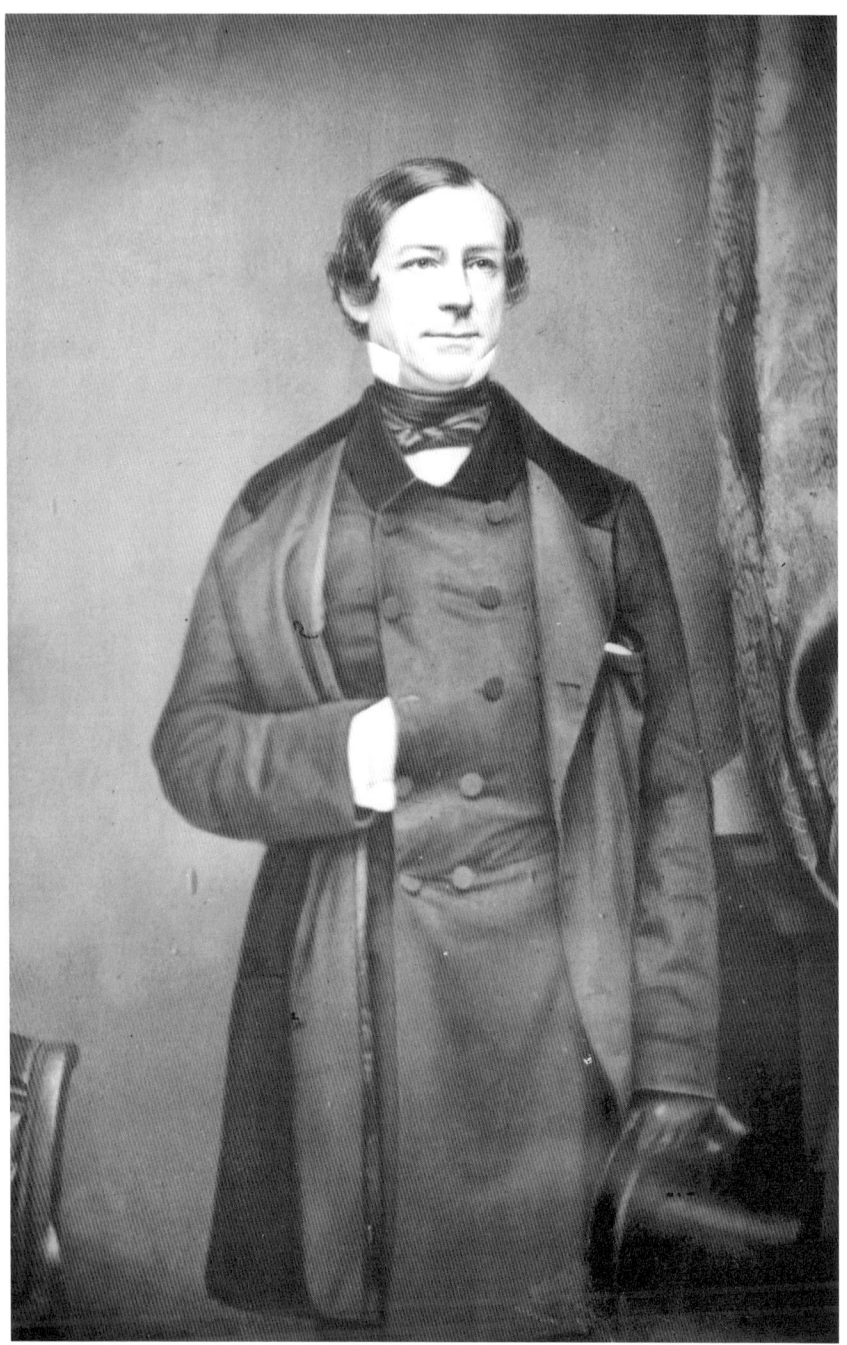
Fernando Wood, United States congressman and two-term mayor of New York. *Library of Congress.*

THE REMARKABLE LIFE OF JOHN MORRISSEY

in Congress, he became a powerful figure in Tammany Hall. He was a man who fit the times perfectly.

Raiding ballot boxes was a practice long associated with New York elections. It was common knowledge that such events helped carry the city for William H. Seward in the state's 1838 gubernatorial election. Five years later, Tammany Hall was guilty of one of the most reprehensible acts of election fraud in American history. The party used its mercenaries to free the convicts at Blackwell Island's penitentiary so they could illegally cast votes. Tammany lodged and fed hundreds of murderers, rapists and thieves and then allowed many of them to escape once they voted as instructed.

John Morrissey was in great demand during these troubled times. Isaiah Rynders assumed Old Smoke would side with the Native Americans as a hired mercenary, but Morrissey detested the Know-Nothings and loathed the ideology supported by men such as Bill Poole. Old Smoke would always be grateful to Rynders for saving his life in the Americus Club, but he was an Irish immigrant and could not stomach siding with the Native Americans no matter how much the pay would be. Morrissey went the opposite route, casting his lot with Tammany Hall. The association would provide him the opportunity to settle some old scores with Poole and his minions, and there were prospects for rapid advancement within the organization.

During Morrissey's California sojourn, Poole had become an even more influential and terrorizing figure on the streets of New York. Born in New Jersey in 1821 to parents of English descent, Poole's family moved to New York in 1831, and his father opened a butcher shop in Manhattan's Washington Market. Bill Poole learned the trade at his father's side and took over the business in the 1840s. Bill the Butcher was always into some sort of nefarious activity. The city's newspapers were filled with tales of Poole's rage. The October 23, 1851 edition of the *New York Times* read:

> *A BRUTAL OUTRAGE ON BROADWAY—We learn that at an early hour yesterday morning, two noted pugilists entered Florence's Hotel, corner of Broadway and Howard Street, and without any provocation seized the bar-keeper and beat his face to a jelly. It appears that Thomas Hyer, William Poole, and several others entered the above hotel, and while one of the party held Charles Owens by the hair of his head, another of the gang beat him in the face to such an extent that his left eye was completely ruined and the flesh of his cheek mangled in the most shocking manner. After thus accomplishing the heartless act, all of them made an effort to find Mr. John Florence, the proprietor of the hotel, with a view of serving*

him in the same manner, but not succeeding in their latter design, they found the hat of Mr. Florence and wantonly cut it into strips, and trampled it under their feet. The desperadoes then left the house, and in the meantime Mr. Owens was placed under medical attendance, and in the course of a short time he proceeded to the Jefferson Market Police, in company with Mr. Florence, where they made their affidavits respecting the inhuman outrage, upon which Justice Blakeley issued his warrants for Hyer, Poole, and such of the others who were concerned in the affair, and the same were placed in the hands of officer Baldwin for service. Since the above was written we have been reliably informed that the affray originated from the fact of the barkeeper having refused them drinks, after they had been furnished with them twice in succession.

As New York's district elections drew near, Poole sought to do everything he could to keep Fernando Wood from climbing the political ladder. Bill the Butcher made no secret of his intention to mount an assault on the polling place at Twenty-third Street and destroy ballots that favored Wood for mayor. Poole, however, couldn't keep his mouth shut about his scheme, and Wood gained knowledge of the plan. Wood needed a man capable of squashing Poole and his gang before they could get to the ballots. Turning to the police was useless. Corrupt aldermen appointed the patrolmen, so it was much wiser for a man such as Wood to hire his own muscle than rely on policemen who went to the highest bidder.

Shortly before the election, John Morrissey received a written request to call on John A. Kennedy, a Tammany supporter and a future New York police superintendent. Old Smoke didn't have any inkling as to what Kennedy wanted, but he showed up to meet him anyway. Upon his arrival, Morrissey saw Kennedy conferring with Fernando Wood. The politician's presence made Old Smoke somewhat uneasy, but he was willing to listen to what the man wanted. Wood informed Morrissey of Bill Poole's plot to pillage the polling place on Twenty-third Street and asked Old Smoke if he would meet Bill the Butcher and his men with a crew of his own. Morrissey told Wood he would do it for free. Old Smoke assured Wood that Poole and his marauders would occupy a row of caskets if they sought any trouble on election day.

Turning to the Dead Rabbits for support, it didn't take Morrissey long to round up fifty men who were as hard as nails to defend the polling station. He armed his warriors with clubs and promised them a dollar each for their efforts. In *The Gangs of New York*, Herbert Asbury stated that Morrissey told his crew that "once a Poole thug had been downed he was to be kept horizontal until his skull was cracked" and that "ears and noses would be highly regarded as souvenirs of an interesting occasion."

Old Smoke covertly positioned his men throughout the polling place. As predicted, Poole and two dozen of his hooligans arrived at noon in a lumber van drawn by four horses. They had no idea what awaited them. As the Know-Nothings entered the building, they were greeted by the menacing John Morrissey and a bloodthirsty crew of brawlers with a significant numbers advantage. Poole, who wasn't expecting any resistance upon his arrival, immediately recognized that he was in over his head on this day. It was a moment to savor for Old Smoke. Bill the Butcher was wise to not make any move that Morrissey would construe as offensive. Poole was fearless, but he knew he lacked the muscle to compete in this particular instance. He wisely ordered his men to retreat. The Tammany ballots had been preserved.

Morrissey accomplished his objective and won a notable victory without having to throw a single punch. The district election, however, did not turn out in Fernando Wood's favor. Even with Old Smoke's assistance, Wood was defeated by the Native American incumbent, Ambrose Kingsland. In the big picture, it was only a minor setback for Wood. He was highly regarded by Tammany Hall and now had an able right-hand man in John Morrissey. The Tammany leadership was most impressed with Morrissey and rewarded him handsomely. The party heavyweights lined Old Smoke's pockets with enough money for him to open his own gambling house with assurances that he would not be impeded by the law. Old Smoke had stood tall against Poole and proved to be a capable general. Battle lines were being drawn.

More than three years had passed since Tom Hyer defeated Yankee Sullivan for the American boxing championship, but Hyer could not be persuaded into defending his title. Hyer insisted he was retired from formal pugilism and never answered any of Morrissey's challenges to step into the ring. This did not sit well with Old Smoke, who continued to taunt Hyer every chance he had. In a card he placed in the *New York Times*, Morrissey said he "never saw a bigger coward in my life" than Hyer and that "what I do say in this article I will say to his face." Morrissey's statement was in response to Hyer challenging him and some of his friends with a pistol. At the time, Morrissey repeated his challenge to settle the matter with fists, but Hyer preferred a gun battle. "I told him that none of my friends were able to fight him, but I was the man," Morrissey said in the *Times*. "His friends were so ashamed of his answer that they left him." Nothing could persuade Hyer to fight Old Smoke. With definitive word that he was retired from the ring, the American boxing championship was vacant. There were two logical successors for the title.

Despite his earlier loss to Hyer, Yankee Sullivan believed he was the best fighter in the land. Morrissey, of course, thought otherwise. After much talk and boasting by each fighter, John Morrissey and Yankee Sullivan agreed to slug it out for $1,000 a side and the vacant championship on October 12, 1853. Old Smoke won a coin flip and was able to determine the location. He selected Boston Corners, a tiny hamlet about one hundred miles north of New York City on the Harlem Railroad.

Physically, Morrissey held every advantage over Sullivan. Old Smoke stood six feet tall and was a chiseled 175 pounds. Sullivan was four inches shorter and weighed approximately 150 pounds. Father Time was also on Morrissey's side. Old Smoke was twenty-two years old, while Sullivan, a veteran of many wars both in and out of the ring, was at least forty. Some accounts of his age stated that Sullivan was as old as forty-two when he fought Morrissey.

Although all the physical attributes and the vitality of youth favored Old Smoke, Sullivan was a skilled fighter with a nasty disposition. Born James Ambrose circa 1811 in County Cork, Ireland, Sullivan was of English descent and spent most of his youth in London before traveling to Australia, where he learned to fight and was constantly in trouble with the law. After finally wearing out his welcome in Australia—he served a small portion of a twenty-year prison sentence at the Botany Bay penal colony before escaping—Sullivan arrived in New York City in the early 1840s and gained a reputation as a prizefighter and political enforcer.

Sullivan continued to make headlines in America. In 1842, he was sentenced to two years in prison for his involvement in the promotion of a fight in New York between Christopher Lilly and Thomas McCoy. The bout resulted in the death of McCoy in the seventy-seventh round after more than two and a half hours of fighting. McCoy's lungs had been punctured during the fight, and he subsequently choked to death on his own blood and bodily fluids. It was the first recorded fatality in an American boxing ring and led to immediate legal response. Robert Morris, New York City's mayor at the time, authorized bounty hunters to track down any persons associated with the fight. A grand jury prosecuted eighteen men on charges ranging from rioting to manslaughter. Sullivan was pardoned after two years behind bars when a fine of $200 was paid on his behalf.

Always the scoundrel, Sullivan liked to engage in river piracy and was known to participate in the occasional armed robbery when his pockets were light. He used a variety of aliases, including Frank Murray and James Sullivan, in an attempt to cloak his illicit activities from the authorities. As a fighter, Sullivan was as seasoned and capable as any man of the era. Even at his advanced age, he was quick and elusive. Sullivan was banking on his considerable ring experience and Morrissey's lack of formal boxing acumen being the difference in the fight.

Old Smoke did the majority of his training at McCombs Dam Park in the Bronx, while Sullivan set up his camp in Brooklyn. The old warrior was constantly insulting Morrissey in public throughout the training period, presuming the style of the fight would ruin Old Smoke's chances. In a rough and tumble—with biting, head butting and eye gouging acceptable tactics—Morrissey would have a decided advantage based on his physical prowess. However, with the rules of the London Prize Ring in effect, Sullivan was convinced he would methodically cut his young adversary to pieces.

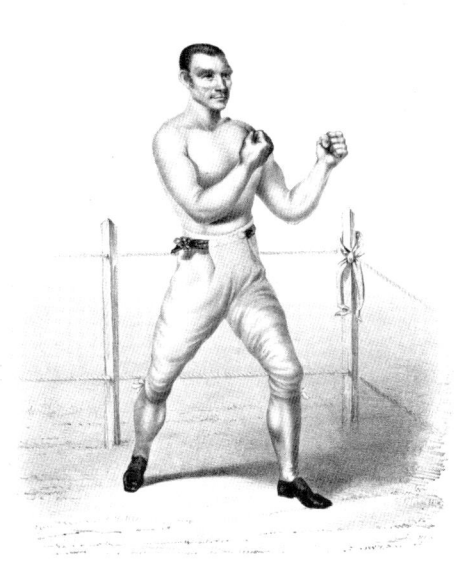

Yankee Sullivan, from a Currier and Ives print. *Library of Congress.*

Morrissey worked himself into top condition and arrived in Boston Corners several days prior to the fight. The buzz surrounding the bout was enormous. Morrissey and Sullivan were both known throughout the country, and talk of the fight was heard in saloons from New York to California. While Sullivan had his share of supporters, the popular opinion was that young Morrissey was simply too big and powerful for Sullivan to contend with. Old Smoke shared those beliefs, confident his heavy hands would batter and bloody Sullivan with ease. The stage was set.

The *New York Herald* described the morning of Wednesday, October 12, 1858, as "clear and crisp…a perfect day for warfare." John Morrissey's opportunity of a lifetime was at hand. The ring was staked in an abandoned brickyard a quarter mile from the Boston Corners stop on the Harlem Railroad. Because the location of the fight was a tiny hamlet on the borders of New York and Massachusetts, it generally went overlooked by law enforcement, making the isolated community an ideal setting for the clandestine affair. Boston Corners, referred to as "Hell's Acres" in some accounts, became a haven for outlaws because it was not policed by either state. Boston Corners was technically part of the Commonwealth of Massachusetts at the time, but its estimated 150 residents never voted in any state election and were not subject to taxation. It was no-man's land. Although it had only one hotel, a single store and a lone blacksmith shop, Boston Corners sat conveniently on the junction of three railroads, including the Harlem, which most New Yorkers used to attend the fight.

Talk of the pending battle was also lively upstate. A large contingent made the journey from Troy to show support for Morrissey. They came by train, horse and covered wagon, descending upon a dot on the map that was not prepared to handle such a crowd. It was estimated that as many as five thousand attended the fight. By eleven o'clock in the morning, the ring was surrounded as anticipation for the biggest fight to date in American history had reached a fever pitch. There were unsavory characters everywhere. The drinking and betting were heavy, and many men were in quarrelsome moods, with pistols at their sides. It was a dangerous and ominous environment.

The fight was delayed for more than two hours while the entourage of each fighter bickered about who would serve as referee. Morrissey was distrustful of the candidates supported by Sullivan and vice versa. There seems, in retrospect, to be no logical reason why such an important detail was not worked out far in advance of the fight, but such was the case. The two sides finally agreed on a man named Charley Allaire to serve as referee. He had no vested interest in either fighter and, more importantly, had prior experience officiating ring battles. The crowd had become agitated by this point, and a hostile environment had developed. It was now one-thirty, and still neither fighter had entered the ring.

A few minutes later, John Morrissey arrived on the scene to thunderous applause. He appeared relaxed and confident as he laughed and exchanged pleasantries with friends and supporters. Old Smoke then made the traditional gesture of throwing his hat in the ring as the crowd hollered its approval. John Morrissey was ready for battle. Old Smoke was accompanied by two "seconds" on this day, Orville "Awful" Gardner and Tom O'Donnell. Gardner, who assisted Morrissey in his training, was a notorious brawler in his own right. Born Hezekiah Orville Gardner in New York City in 1825, Gardner was the most ruthless of five brothers who all had a fighting reputation of some degree. One of Awful's brothers also had a colorful nickname, Howell "the Horrible" Gardner.

Awful Gardner spent much of his youth in Newark, New Jersey, but fled back to the city of his birth after killing a man in a street fight. Like Morrissey, Gardner became an immigrant runner and sought glory as a pugilist. Gardner earned some fistic fame with a victory in thirty-three rounds against Allen McFee in 1849, but his ring career stalled after that. He became increasingly notorious for street fighting, gambling and drinking. The *New York Times* referred to him as "Mr. Awful," and accounts of his thuggish behavior filled the pages of the New York rags. One incident in 1852 reported in the *Times* described a brawl in which Mr. Awful pummeled several patrons at the Oyster Saloon. In the mêlée, Gardner was said to have maimed one man by biting off his nose and one of his ears. Although his own career as a boxer never amounted to much, Gardner was a significant presence at John Morrissey's side.

Old Smoke played to the crowd as he awaited the entrance of Yankee Sullivan. Gardner proudly tied Morrissey's colors—a scarf decorated with the American Stars and Stripes—to one of the ring stakes. The crowd again shouted its approval for Old Smoke. As Morrissey put a charge into the mob, Sullivan began to elbow his way through the drunken mass of humanity as he jogged toward the ring. With Andy Sheehan on one side and "Admiral" Billy Wilson on the other, Sullivan displayed a menacing snarl as he entered the ring. Wilson then wrapped Sullivan's colors to an opposite ring stake. The all-black handkerchief, in the tradition of bare-knuckle brawling, signified victory or death.

The physical difference in the combatants was striking. Old Smoke looked like an extraordinary specimen next to the weathered Sullivan. There was no doubt Morrissey owned the advantages of size, strength and youth, but Sullivan boasted speed, elusiveness and the ring science his inexperienced foe lacked. Each man had an umpire who could advocate to the referee to make sure that the rules of the London Prize Ring were being fairly enforced. Morrissey's umpire was John Devoe, while Sullivan had none other than Bill Poole in his corner. Poole didn't particularly care for Sullivan, but he detested Morrissey from their first encounter in the Americus Club and was willing to aid any man who sought to batter Old Smoke.

Once all the pre-fight rituals were concluded, the two combatants placed themselves in traditional fighting portraits in the center of the ring. Time was signaled, and the championship bout commenced at seven minutes before two o'clock in the afternoon. One of the most hyped encounters in the history of American pugilism was finally underway.

Morrissey wasn't interested in waiting for Sullivan to engage him. As he did against George Thompson in California, Old Smoke charged Sullivan immediately. Unleashing wild haymakers with both hands, Morrissey found nothing but air. Sullivan showed he was as quick as a cat and darted around the ring unscathed early. Following Old Smoke's initial misses, Sullivan connected with a stabbing left hand that opened a gash on the young slugger's right cheek. It had taken less than a minute for Old Smoke to realize that Yankee Sullivan was a man to be reckoned with. As blood streamed from his cheek, Morrissey moved quickly to deliver a response. Once again, Old Smoke came up empty. Sullivan jumped back to evade the blow and slipped to the ground to end the round.

Sullivan's stick-and-move strategy was proving effective. Old Smoke was frustrated with the tactics. Morrissey, however, was stubborn and refused to make adjustments. He continued to swing outrageously in hopes of connecting on some heavy shots that would wear down Sullivan and slow his rapid movements. The early rounds were dominated by Sullivan. He would hit and run before diving to the ground to avoid danger whenever Old Smoke closed in. Morrissey continued in his efforts to corner Sullivan. He knew he could inflict substantial damage if he was able to trap him against the ropes or a post. Morrissey's face was frightfully carved up by the end of the fourth round. He had a swollen eye, and blood was drizzling from his nose and cheek. His face and chest were a dark coat of smeared crimson. The betting odds at ringside were now $100 to $75 in favor of Sullivan. Old Smoke was in great danger of both losing the fight and being embarrassed. Yankee Sullivan was that good.

Morrissey had his first glimmer of hope in the fifth round. Sullivan continued to hit and run, but Old Smoke finally got his opponent in a corner and uncoiled a wicked right hand that cracked Sullivan in the ribs. Morrissey then connected with a sensational shot to Sullivan's jaw. Sullivan's legs buckled, and he hit the dirt hard. Old Smoke's supporters finally had reason to rejoice. Sullivan slowly made his way to his feet and wobbled to his corner. Morrissey's raw power was incredible, and Sullivan still seemed dazed as the sixth round opened. Old Smoke had sapped some of the bounce from Sullivan's legs and was starting to become more accurate with his knuckles. Morrissey closed the sixth round with another powerful knockdown of Sullivan. This time, he successfully targeted Sullivan's neck with a right hook.

Morrissey had weathered a tremendous storm and was now in the fight. He was bloodied and his face was swollen, but he had not gone down and seemed to be turning the tide. Sullivan, however, came to scratch for the seventh round revitalized. Amazingly, he seemed to have recovered much of his quickness and went right back to the stick-and-move tactics that proved so successful in the early rounds. Sullivan was again landing slashing shots to Morrissey's face and body and ducking to the ground whenever Old Smoke threatened to corner him. This went on for several rounds, and Sullivan again seized control of the fight. He was dictating the tempo and irritating Morrissey with his tactics.

Old Smoke absorbed an incredible amount of punishment, but he never backed down and never went down. Morrissey was enduring a dreadful beating, but he was in this for the long haul. In his corner, Gardner and O'Donnell barked at referee Charley Allaire about Sullivan taking dives, but Allaire knew the rules of the ring and reiterated to Old Smoke's seconds that a man had the right to go down and end a round whether he was giving or taking a blow. The crowd was grumbling and growing restless as the rounds passed and Sullivan continued to have success. He was masterfully executing his plan with patience and precision.

Morrissey stubbornly continued to begin each round with a bull rush at Sullivan in an attempt to turn the old man's lights out. Each time he came up empty. The veteran repeatedly ducked and dodged the young fighter's fists. Although his face was a grotesque sight and he was taking considerable punishment, Old Smoke's legs were steady and his iron body was holding up quite well. Sullivan, meanwhile, began to wear down. As the bout passed the thirtieth round, Sullivan's punches were no longer as crisp as they were earlier in the fight and his legs became heavy. For as much punishment as he had dished out, Sullivan was never able to knock Morrissey to the dirt.

The thirty-seventh round of the Morrissey-Sullivan title fight remains one of the most controversial in the history of American boxing. Sullivan opened the round with a dull swing and miss. Morrissey cornered his fading opponent and threw him hard against one of the ring's stakes. Old Smoke closed in and thumped Sullivan with a vicious series of blows in an attempt to end the proceedings. A desperate Sullivan clinched Old Smoke in a last-gasp attempt to avoid defeat. Morrissey responded by bullying Sullivan back into the ropes. He grabbed Sullivan's neck with his left hand to hold his head steady while pulverizing his skull with a series of rights.

There was nothing in the rules that prohibited choking an opponent. The tactic was as perfectly legal as Sullivan dropping to the ground to avoid punishment. Old Smoke cracked Sullivan's head with one devastating hammer shot after another. Recognizing their fighter was nearing his end, "Admiral Billy" Wilson and Andy Sheehan rushed into the ring, and mayhem ensued. Morrissey then lifted Sullivan into the air and slammed him to the ground.

In response to Sullivan's men entering the ring, Awful Gardner and Tom O'Donnell also joined the mêlée. The championship fight had become a scene of pandemonium. Numerous incensed and drunken spectators climbed into the ring, and chaos followed for several minutes. Old Smoke was punching Billy Wilson, while Sullivan, who was badly beaten and barely standing, was occupied with none other than Awful Gardner. After the riot simmered down and the ring was cleared, referee Charley Allaire signaled for the fighters to come to scratch for a thirty-eighth round. Morrissey answered the call and made his way to the center of the ring. What happened with Sullivan is the subject of much debate and varying accounts. Some stories contend Sullivan decided he could take no more punishment from Old Smoke and refused to continue. Other versions state that Sullivan was too busy slugging it out with Awful Gardner and ignored the call to scratch. What is certain is Sullivan did not continue and Allaire raised Morrissey's hand as the winner and new American boxing champion. Thus ended one of the fiercest bare-knuckle bouts ever fought in the United States.

Showing tremendous courage and a cast-iron jaw, John Morrissey had taken Yankee Sullivan's best shots pressed forward each time. He never tasted the dirt beneath him and in the end was thrashing his adversary. The decision to award the fight to Morrissey was met with controversy in some circles, but it was clear Old Smoke had seized control of the fight before the free-for-all erupted in the ring. John Morrissey had proven to be a most exceptional bare-knuckle warrior and one of the most resilient men to ever step into a ring. In a *New York Times* account, Sullivan said of Morrissey, "You might as well hit a brick wall as hit that man on the head."

What happened following the fight sadly became known as "the Sack of Millerton." As the controversial title bout concluded, an ensuing riot among the spectators spilled out of the brickyard and into neighboring farms and nearby communities. The rioters began to pillage farms and residences and raid pantries for food and liquor. They slaughtered hogs and roasted them along the roadside in a drunken state. Boston Corners, Millerton and other nearby communities were decimated by the thousands of marauders. Various contemporary reports said the fightgoers stripped residences of every edible thing and caused widespread property destruction. Some of the terrorized locals managed to flag down a passing train to flee the area.

Law enforcement eventually received word of the disgraceful aftermath and moved in to restore order. The only person they managed to arrest was Yankee Sullivan, who was tracked down in Lenox, Massachusetts. Morrissey, meanwhile, escaped through the Taconic Hills and made his way back to New York City. Old Smoke, the new American boxing champion, eventually paid a small fine for "participating in an illegal prizefight," but Sullivan remained in jail, unable to afford bail.

The sportsmen of New York and several of Sullivan's friends didn't want to see him languish in a cell after he fought so valiantly against Morrissey. Tom Hyer, who defeated Sullivan three years earlier, helped raise the necessary funds to secure the bail. Even Morrissey contributed to the cause. Sullivan decided not to stick around. He headed to the West Coast looking for new opportunities and was never seen in New York again.

The infamous championship spectacle made a national sensation of John Morrissey and also changed tiny Boston Corners forever. The events that took place after the fight drove the area's residents to petition the United States Congress to bring the village under the jurisdiction of the State of New York. On January 3, 1855, an act of Congress officially changed the state line and made Boston Corners a part of New York.

STREETS OF BLOOD

At the ripe old age of twenty-two, John Morrissey was enjoying a grand life full of adventure. His victory over Yankee Sullivan gave him much more than the American boxing championship. The notoriety Morrissey garnered from defeating Sullivan convinced John Petrie to make him a partner in his New York gambling houses. Teaming with Petrie quickly made Old Smoke a wealthy man. Petrie understood Morrissey's vast appeal as a drawing card. Men of all walks of life—gutter brawlers, river pirates, politicians and even society's aristocrats—desired to rub elbows with the champion. Business was good for both Petrie and Morrissey.

Another contributing factor in the success Old Smoke enjoyed with Petrie was the fact that they ran honest table games. Few of New York's gambling halls could make such a claim. Morrissey and Petrie believed that players who knew they were getting an honest shake would become loyal patrons. Their integrity reaped them a sizeable financial windfall.

A champion fighter with a big bankroll, John Morrissey had much to be pleased about. Now that he had made something of himself, Old Smoke believed the time was right to ask Susie Smith for her hand in marriage. Convincing her father, the gruff steamboat captain, would not be easy. Although Captain Smith liked Morrissey, he was also a protective father who saw the dark side and rage of Old Smoke. Captain Smith knew Morrissey lived a life that was perpetually on the cusp of danger. Although he feared for his daughter in a life such as this, Captain Smith also recognized that the young brute he first knew as a deckhand on the *City of Troy* had worked tirelessly to gain Susie's love and trust. Captain Smith eventually gave his blessing for John and Susie to wed.

John Morrissey was on top of the world. He was about to be married and was revered as a titan in the sporting world. Money was flowing in through his gambling interests, and he was becoming an influential figure in New York politics. It was a life just about any Irishman from Morrissey's origins could only dream of. For Old Smoke, however, the restlessness in his soul was always difficult to satisfy. It was nothing a little mischief couldn't cure. After all, it seemed an appropriate time to celebrate all the fortune of a good life.

Morrissey was a regular drinker, as were most men he associated with, but he rarely lost control of his actions. One such lapse from sobriety, however, almost proved extremely costly. A month prior to his wedding, Morrissey rounded up his closest friends for a grand celebration. Dad Cunningham and John Petrie were among the crew joining the champion for the festivities. They started early one morning at the Bull's Head Tavern for a customary breakfast of steak, toast, potatoes, eggs and coffee. The lavish feast was accompanied by iced buckets of wine, which were quickly consumed by Old Smoke and his comrades. It was the beginning of a long day of drinking and foolishness.

As the bender wore on, Morrissey and his cronies eventually slipped under the haze of the booze. One by one, they called it a day as each reached the limit of his functionality. Everyone except Old Smoke. Morrissey knew no limits on this day. He was a drunken mess, but he meant to press on. This was a day to celebrate, and the champion was doing just that. Old Smoke wobbled into the bar at the Girard House. Alone, inebriated and becoming quarrelsome, he staggered up to the bar and demanded a whisky. Observing the poor condition Old Smoke was in, the bartender refused to serve him. Morrissey went into a rage. He smashed his hand on the counter and repeated his demand to be served. Again, he was refused. The bartender attempted as best he could to appease Old Smoke, but it was to no avail. Morrissey had reached a boiling point, and there was no reasoning with him. Recognizing the dangerous champion was about to erupt, the bartender signaled to a pair of burly bouncers in an effort to calm the storm that Morrissey had become.

As the bouncers closed in, Old Smoke raised his fists and prepared for combat. One of the bouncers slipped behind Morrissey and wrapped his arms around the champion. Old Smoke quickly broke loose and flung the man to the floor. The drunken Morrissey then reached into his jacket, pulled out a pistol and took aim at one of the bouncers. The situation had gone from dangerous to deadly in an instant. Old Smoke seemed intent on killing a man in cold blood.

Fortunately for all parties involved, several policemen poured into the Girard House just as Morrissey drew his pistol. They swarmed Old Smoke and managed to wrestle the drunken brawler to the ground. Refusing to yield, Morrissey battered several officers before he was finally restrained and hauled off to jail. Word of Old Smoke's shameful behavior soon reached Captain Smith and Susie. Old Smoke's celebration had become a nightmare. He had almost killed a man in a drunken deluge, and everything he had fought so hard for was now in jeopardy as his head pounded in a jail cell.

Although he was remorseful, Morrissey didn't believe he had much to be concerned with from a legal standpoint. He assumed his political connections would make the incident go away and that it would quickly be forgotten. That was not the case. To his dismay, Old Smoke was not released right away, and charges of assault with intent to kill were filed with the court. Bail was set in the amount of $2,000. Petrie arrived on the scene and forked over the money to provide Morrissey temporary freedom. Old Smoke's enemies were conspiring against him. The Know-Nothings were doing everything they could politically to make sure the case against the champion fighter had legs. It was widely speculated that Morrissey would have to serve time in prison, an outcome he was desperate to avoid. He knew that if he were to be incarcerated, no matter the length of the term, Captain Smith would never permit him to marry his daughter and his relationship with Susie would be in jeopardy.

Old Smoke appealed to the district attorney, A. Oakley Hall. A future mayor of New York, Hall was known to waver in his political allegiances for the right price. There was tremendous pressure provided by the Know-Nothings in an effort to keep Morrissey locked up and off the streets, but at the same time Hall knew there would be even greater outrage among the Dead Rabbits and Tammany Hall's inner circle if Old Smoke served any time. After much wrangling, Hall saw to it that the case was indefinitely delayed and eventually dropped.

Susie Smith was predictably sickened by Morrissey's actions, but Old Smoke pleaded with her and she eventually agreed to forgive him. Captain Smith was much more difficult to pacify. His daughter was a beautiful, intelligent young woman who deserved better than a violent thug for a husband, but Susie was not going to walk away from Morrissey, and the wedding finally took place. It was a modest ceremony with only a few friends in attendance at the Smith family home in Troy. John Morrissey realized he

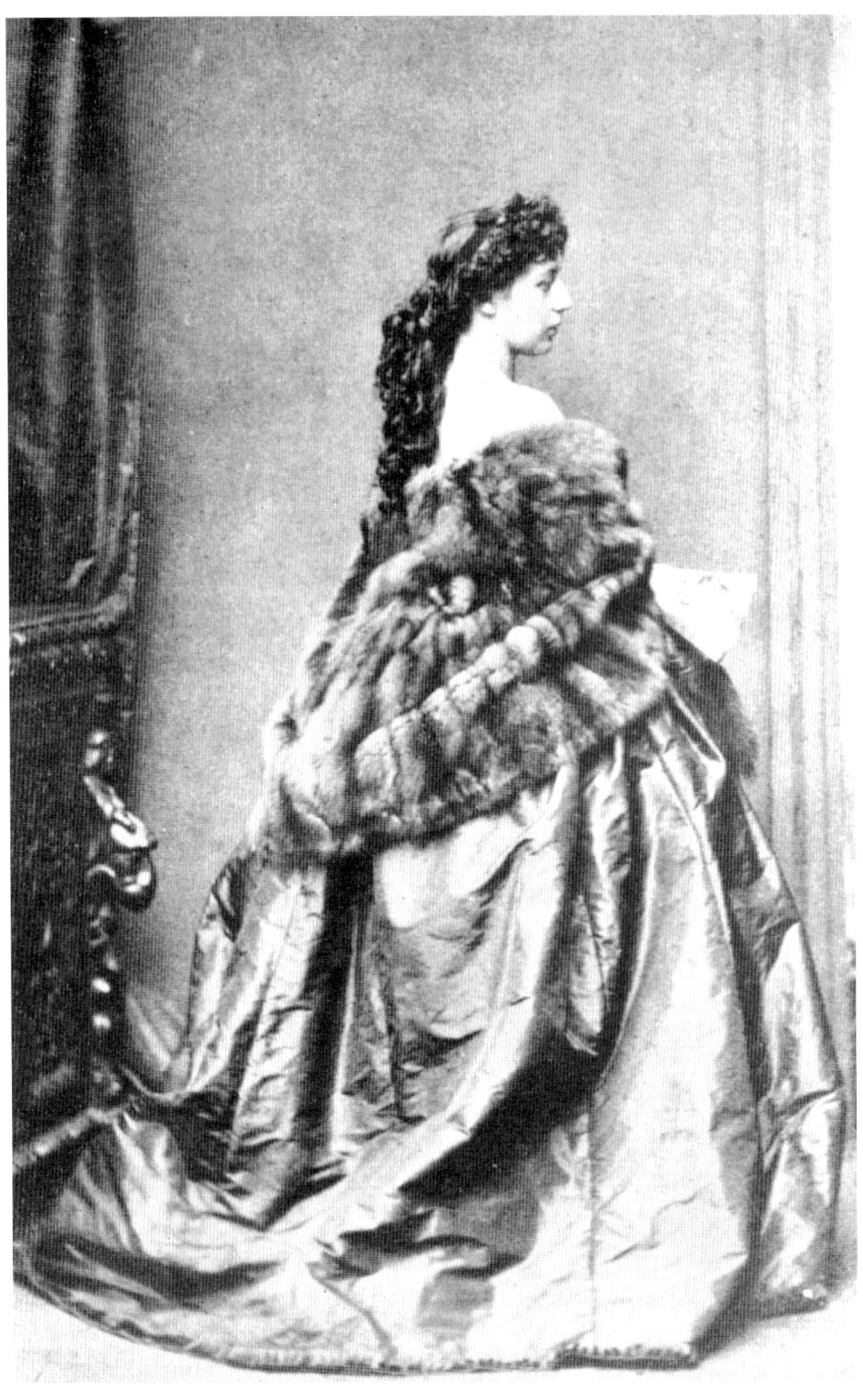

Mrs. John Morrissey. *New York State Museum Archives*.

was a fortunate man. Susie Smith would have been justified if she decided to walk away in the aftermath of Old Smoke's terrible lapse of judgment. Susie, however, was both loyal and forgiving and believed any rough edges in Morrissey's character could be smoothed out.

Mr. and Mrs. John Morrissey purchased a home in New York City on Hudson Street and took in Captain Smith, who was getting old and struggling with his mobility. Old Smoke's carefree existence was now a thing of the past. He was a family man with responsibilities. He had a wife and a father-in-law to care for, a home and certain expectations to meet. None of his newfound responsibilities, however, would mean that John Morrissey was about to lead a simple or safe life. Old Smoke was a man of action and a violent individual in a violent time.

Morrissey remained quite busy after his wedding. He split his time between tending to his gambling interests and political duties on behalf of Tammany Hall's Fernando Wood, who eyed becoming New York's mayor. Wood didn't have all of Tammany's support, however, as the party was experiencing plenty of internal strife. The Native Americans were busy searching for their own candidate, while the City Reformers were plotting an affiliation with the Whigs. Wood faced the challenge of unifying the divided factions within Tammany. In this task, Morrissey played a key role as counsel to Wood.

While the Whigs and City Reformers never agreed on terms of an alliance, one of the Tammany factions backed Augustus Schell for mayor. Schell hailed from one of the city's oldest and most influential families, and he was regarded as one of the finest lawyers in New York. The Know-Nothings pushed James W. Baker, an auctioneer, as their candidate, while the Whigs supported John J. Herrick, a commission merchant. Meanwhile, the upstart City Reformers endorsed Wilson G. Hunt, a dealer in cloth.

Wood was interested in strengthening his foothold by seeking the backing of the Know-Nothings. Morrissey vehemently opposed this strategy, recognizing that an alliance between the Irish immigrants who supported Tammany Hall in great numbers would never accept a candidate who pandered to the Native Americans. Morrissey convinced Wood to cast his lot with the Irishmen. He figured the strength of their numbers would put Wood in the mayor's seat if he was willing to condemn the Know-Nothings and their anti-immigrant beliefs. Morrissey's street sense proved to be a valuable commodity for Wood. Old Smoke believed he could deliver the Irish vote, but Wood had plenty of detractors and nothing was certain. Although he preached improved living conditions, better jobs and social equality for the poor immigrants in New York, Wood was ridiculed by the *New York Times* on election day in 1854. The *Times* stated:

> *Fernando Wood, the regular nominee of the Soft Shells, is known to be utterly unfit for the place. His integrity as a business man has been seriously impeached by the publication of legal testimony, the truth of which does not seem to be controverted, and which is conclusive against his fitness for any place of trust and responsibility. He has published a card and it is said made an affidavit denouncing the Know-Nothings and denying in the most explicit terms that he has any connection with the order. And yet it is known to thousands of our citizens that he has been a member of the order and acted as one of its Executive Committee. The fact that he has since resigned and that, in a technical sense, his assertions may be true does not in the least relieve him of the odium of* intending *to deceive. No such man ought to be trusted in any office, and it would be a disgrace to the city to elect him Mayor. If those who are convinced of this were united in their opposition, his defeat would be beyond all doubt. Unfortunately, this is not the case.*

Prior to the election, Morrissey convinced Wood to distribute propaganda cards throughout the city in an effort to portray the candidate favorably to the immigrants who did not know his political record or past ties to the Know-Nothings. Wood claimed to be a champion of the common man and made promises of sweeping reforms to help the poor. While not convincing everyone, especially the watchful *Times*, the strategy proved to be an effective one. Old Smoke also helped Wood naturalize more than three thousand men on the eve of the election by sending them to a Tammany-friendly judge with preprinted voting cards requesting what amounted to a rubber stamp as a personal courtesy. The numbers on election day were not overwhelming for Wood, but they were more than sufficient. He received 19,664 of the overall 59,664 votes, enough to elect him New York's mayor. Morrissey had done his part and was now in a position of tremendous influence.

Wood's victory—and Old Smoke's contributions to it—incensed Bill Poole and the Know-Nothings. Morrissey happened to be at the bar of the City Hotel one night in February 1855 when Poole sauntered in. Theodore Allen, a former assistant in Poole's butcher market and a supporter of the Know-Nothings, penned the following account of the confrontation and its aftermath for the *Police Gazette*:

THE REMARKABLE LIFE OF JOHN MORRISSEY

Morrissey was standing at the bar as Poole entered and advanced toward him. The place was full of people and all talk died down until there was not even a whisper. The two eyed each other with cold alertness. Morrissey was first to speak.

"There stands the black-muzzled American fighter," Old Smoke said with a tone of defiance.

"Yes," responded Poole with a mischievous smile, "and I'm a dandy."

"I can lick all the dandy out of you tomorrow morning," Morrissey countered. "What is more, I'll bet you five thousand dollars you don't dare meet me, and you can name the place." And he put fifty dollars as a forfeit in the hands of George Deagle, chief clerk of the hotel.

"How about the foot of Christopher Street?" asked Poole. He had named a location within a couple blocks of his own home.

Tom Burns, one of Morrissey's supporters in the bar, protested and shouted out:

"Don't go there, John, that's Poole's headquarters. His gang will never let you get away alive."

After a moment's hesitation, Morrissey tossed over fifty dollars to Poole and dared him to name another place.

"How will the Amos Street dock suit you?" asked Bill the Butcher.

"That's satisfactory," was the bold answer, though Amos was but a block removed from Christopher.

"I'll be there bright and early," Poole said.

Five o' clock in the morning Poole came up to the dock in a coach accompanied by "Smut" Ackerman, Tommy Culkin and myself. Numerous admirers of Poole had already put in appearance, and had cleared a place for the fight and were camped out. As there was a nipping coolness in the air on this February morning Bill decided to warm up by enjoying a bit of exercise. Accompanied by a couple of his boon companions and myself he rowed across the river to Barker's Gardens, a resort in Hoboken, near the ferry. There we had a few drinks, Poole calling for his favorite, milk punch. He took his turn at the oars on the way back to limber up. We pulled into the Hammond Street dock and then left Bill to rest in the Village House, while I went down the street to see if the enemy had put in appearance.

Morrissey had not yet got uptown. A number of his friends, however, had started up Hudson Street in coaches. Poole's friends were lying in wait for them and every carriage that appeared was stopped and either upset or emptied of its inmates. A fight invariable [sic] ensued, which ended in Old Smoke's supporters making their departure for home or a hospital.

BARE KNUCKLES & SARATOGA RACING

It was 7 A.M. before news, which traveled ahead of him, apprised that Morrissey was driving up with a friend in a light wagon. I had time to get Poole to the wharf before John arrived. He came with Johnny Lyng, proprietor of the Sportsman's Headquarters, at Canal Street and Broadway, and they walked toward us arm in arm. The crowd which swarmed on the dock made a lane for them to pass through and everything was very orderly. Even the hundreds who crowded the roofs and windows of the adjacent buildings were quiet. But among the people on the pier was John Poole, Bill's brother. He had undergone a frightful mauling in Lyng's place and burned for revenge. Bill's brother struck his enemy a smashing blow on the jaw. In a second there was a general fight. No one attempted to molest Morrissey, who stood quietly looking on. But his followers fared badly. They were given a thorough thrashing, their revolvers taken from them and they were tossed into the river. After this delay the principals were permitted to get to business.

There was no ring, but by general consent the throng kept a space open for the combat. Poole in his undershirt, as he had rowed across the river, was ready. It did not take Morrissey long to peel. Throwing off his coat and white shirt, he stood in his red flannel undershirt, as brawny a young bruiser as the most enthusiastic admirer of muscle could desire to see.

The fight began with some light sparring. Poole holding himself principally on the defensive as his opponent circled about for a chance to close. For about five minutes this child's play of the giants lasted. Then Morrissey made a rush.

Clutching each other in grips of steel they butted and pounded their heads and bodies together, tearing at each other's face with their teeth and gouging for eyes with talon-like finger. It was sickening to watch, for in no time they were frightfully punished. There was a long gash in Poole's cheeks where the flesh had been torn by his opponent's teeth. Blood was streaming from Morrissey's eyes.

The crowd closed in on them and the surging bodies of the combatants pressed against the feet and legs of the surrounding onlookers. The wonder is that the two on the ground were saved from being trampled to death. But Morrissey was underneath and doomed to defeat.

"I'm satisfied," he gasped. "I'm done."

During the mêlée, Poole had Morrissey pinned down, and according to another account, Poole's henchmen ensured that Old Smoke would suffer. Ed James of the *Clipper*, one of the most respected newspapermen of the day, wrote, "A number of Poole's partisans joined in and hammered and kicked Morrissey while he lay upon the ground until the wonder was he was not killed."

There were several accounts of what transpired at the Amos Street dock that morning. In *The Gangs of New York*, Herbert Asbury reported that Poole never even appeared on the scene and that two hundred of his men ambushed Morrissey and a small group of his supporters. Morrissey published his version of the events in the *New York Times*:

> *When I started from my house to go and fight Poole, I was alone, but little did I think that Poole had a hundred men on the ground stripped to help whip me. When I arrived at Amos Street, I know I was obliged to be whipped. I, however, went down to the dock and met Poole. As we squared off, all of Poole's friends (for nobody else was there) surrounded me. I then turned toward them and said, "Sit down, and you all can see the fight." At this time a dozen of the hounds broke out and exclaimed, "We will do as we please." I then said to them, "Why all of you don't want to murder me, do you?" I then hit Poole, and no sooner than I had given the blow, I was struck by some half a dozen persons standing at my back. Poole then clenched me, but did not throw me as was erroneously stated in the papers. The crowd then seized hold of me and pulled me down. At the time we fell, his friends commenced kicking me in the face and yelled "Kill him." Poole never hit me a single blow, but bit me in the cheek. I looked around to see if I knew anybody there. I did not see any one but Poole's friends, who were engaged in kicking me...After I rose to me feet, Poole's friends again hit me several times. When I started to go to the foot of Amos Street, I supposed that fair play would be shown me in the fight with Poole, but instead of that I was ferociously assailed by the entire mob, and I without a friend. Notwithstanding the violence that was used toward me by the mob, I am ready to fight Bill Poole within 48 hours, and I will fight him any way he chooses to name, and at any place, barring Amos Street or any portion of that locality where his cowardly gang holds out. However, I am of the opinion that Poole is too big a coward to fight me fairly at any other place.*

Fair of foul, Poole had apparently gotten the best of Old Smoke on this day. A couple weeks later, on the night of February 24, 1855, Morrissey ran into Poole and several of his supporters at Stanwix Hall, one of New York's most popular saloons. Bill the Butcher was about to engage in a fight with Mark Maguire, one of Morrissey's supporters, when detective Chris Hogan intervened. At that moment, Old Smoke entered the barroom and whipped out a pistol. Morrissey took aim at Bill the Butcher, and Poole's minions promptly scattered. Old Smoke pulled the trigger, but the hammer jammed and he tossed the gun to the floor. The following exchange was reported by the *Police Gazette*:

> "You always was lucky," Morrissey said.
> The Butcher's miasmic eyes glittered. He reached over the free-lunch counter, seized two carving knives and hurled them point first into the bar.
> "There, you son of a bitch!" Poole shouted. "Take your pick. I'll fight you with them."
> "Do you think I'm a fool? Knives are for butchers like you to slit dead pigs with," Morrissey said. "I've seen you throw one through an inch of pine at twenty feet. You've got hands. You brag about being great with them. Let's see."

Detective Hogan had slipped out of the bar and returned with a dozen officers ready to arrest Morrissey and Poole. After cooler heads prevailed, at least temporarily, both men were allowed to leave as long as they agreed to go home. Old Smoke returned to his house on Hudson Street, but Bill the

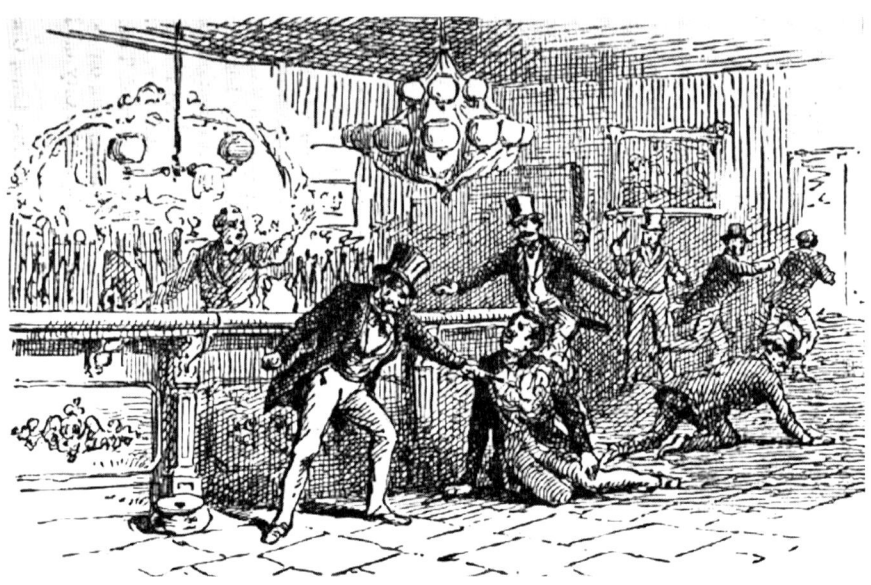

Depiction of the murder of "Bill the Butcher" Poole at Stanwix Hall, 1855. *From* Frank Leslie's Illustrated Newspaper.

THE REMARKABLE LIFE OF JOHN MORRISSEY

Butcher sought additional action. Poole returned to Stanwix Hall a couple hours later that night with a pair of thugs at his side. A short time later, Morrissey supporters Lew Baker, Jim Turner and Paugeen McLaughlin entered the bar and locked the door behind them.

Turner took aim at Poole with a pistol and shot him in the leg. Bill the Butcher crashed to the ground. Baker and McLaughlin proceeded to thrash Poole's men, Charley Lozier and Cy Shay, who fled the establishment. Baker bent over Poole, who was crawling toward the bar in an attempt to grab a carving knife.

"I guess I'll take you," Baker said to Poole before firing two slugs into Bill the Butcher's chest.

Shay ran to the closest police station. Poole, covered in blood and barely clinging to life, was taken to his home on Christopher Street. By the following morning, Tuner and McLaughlin had been arrested, but Baker had escaped across the river to Jersey City. The shooting of Poole was the most discussed topic in the city. Bulletins of his condition were issued hourly. Poole remarkably hung on for two weeks before finally succumbing to his wounds. He died on March 8, 1855, at the age of thirty-three. Only a few minutes before expiring, Bill the Butcher famously remarked, "Goodbye boys…I die a true American."

FIGHT OF THE CENTURY

Because of his known hatred for Bill Poole and the earlier events at Stanwix Hall the night of February 24, 1855, John Morrissey was arrested and charged as an accessory in Bill the Butcher's murder. Lew Baker was eventually tracked down and tried along with Jim Turner and Paugeen McLaughlin for the actual killing. After three juries were hung, the authorities dropped the case, and all involved were released. Morrissey's charge as an accessory never went to court. Baker left for France, and Turner moved to California following his release. McLaughlin stuck around New York, but he was shot and killed in 1858 by Dad Cunningham over a dispute in a dice game.

No evidence was ever presented that Morrissey arranged Poole's murder or that he had a role in the rioting that occurred at Bill the Butcher's funeral. Theodore Allen's description of the latter event in the *Police Gazette* stated:

> *The sidewalks all along the route of the procession were jammed. The very trees, awnings and projecting signs were seized on as points of vantage, and the air was alive with the great roar of the multitude. Opposite the dead man's residence was a shop owned by a carpenter named Onderdonk. It was a sturdy two-story frame building with a stairway on the outside giving access to the upper floor. The spectators packed this stairway in a solid mass, and every inch of roof space was also taken up. The structure began to creak ominously, and then the roof and stairs gave way, and people and timbers fell together in one common wreck. Four were killed and thirty injured.*

> *Amid this confusion the funeral cortege got under way. It was headed by a detail of several hundred of the old police force. The van of the procession was led by the Poole Association, some two thousand strong. Then came deputations from the order of United Americans from various cities forming a body twice as great. The famous Shiffler House of Philadelphia followed with about one thousand members, and various local and visiting companies, headed by the Red Rover, Engine No. 34, of which Poole had been a member. Then came thousands of citizens in advance of the hearse, which was guarded by two companies named in the dead man's honor.*
>
> *The course lay through Christopher and Bleecker Streets on to Broadway. At Grand Street a body of five hundred men in familiar garb of working butchers knelt with their heads uncovered as the procession passed. They fell in and accompanied the march to the ferry. The funeral and its immediate escort continued on to Greenwood Cemetery in Brooklyn, where Bill Poole was committed to the last long rest.*
>
> *After the ceremony the procession broke up. The Poole and the Light Guards marched together and reached Broadway and Canal Street, where the New York and New Haven depot occupied one corner. Opposite the depot a house was being torn down. Behind the brick and timber barricade, a strong party of Morrissey followers had gathered. They consisted of members of the 36th Engine known as the Original Hounds, reinforced by a gang of Dead Rabbits.*
>
> *As the Poole volunteers came within range a volley of stones and bricks darkened the air. The attack was so unforeseen that spectators who were gathered in the street watching the parade had no time to get out of the way. Shouts and screams and cheers made a ringing chorus through which was heard the crack of pistols and the smash of stoned crashing windows… The fighting continued for an hour until the Seventh Regiment appeared to suppress the riot. Bill Poole's burial had been a grand and exciting occasion!*

With his deadliest rival now in the ground, Old Smoke continued to grow in political power. Susie Morrissey hoped her husband would now turn his attention to safer activities and leave the gangland lifestyle behind. Morrissey's wife continued to press the issue, especially after the birth of their child, John Morrissey Jr., on August 6, 1855. Fighting, however, was in Old Smoke's soul. He made his way in the world with his fists and was not ready to retire them just yet.

Organized fights were infrequent during the bare-knuckle era. Tom Hyer had an eight-year gap between winning the American championship against

THE REMARKABLE LIFE OF JOHN MORRISSEY

Country McCloskey and defending the title versus Yankee Sullivan. After defeating Sullivan in 1853, John Morrissey did not have a worthy challenger for his crown until five years later. It would be an enemy he knew well.

During his formative years in Troy, Morrissey became friends with another young tough named John Camel Heenan. Morrissey's family socialized regularly with the Heenans, who also came to America from Templemore. The families were friends for years until a feud developed between the boys' fathers that stemmed from a disagreement involving their partnership in fighting cocks. Blows were exchanged, and the stubborn men never spoke again.

John Morrissey was three years older than John Heenan, but the boys knew each other well growing up. They worked together at a stove company and even fought in the same gang for a time before Morrissey went to New York City. A few years later, young John Heenan ventured west and found work with the Pacific Steamship Company, located in Benicia, California. Heenan and Morrissey were similar in many ways. The common upbringing led both to develop quick tempers and solve problems with their fists. As Morrissey did, Heenan likewise made his pugilistic debut in California. The six-foot-two Heenan was arguably even more physically prolific than Morrissey. He packed two hundred pounds onto his frame, which was hardened and chiseled by wielding sledgehammers and working with other heavy equipment for the Pacific Steamship Company. Heenan pulverized several foes in informal bouts in California and was making quite a name for himself. Dubbed the "Benicia Boy," Heenan was big, powerful, intimidating and hungry for an opportunity.

While in California, Heenan was discovered by a cantankerous English trainer named Jim Cusick, who convinced him to return to New York and make a name for himself. Heenan made his New York fighting debut on December 10, 1857, against the highly regarded Joe Coburn. Heenan easily defeated his overmatched foe, and discussion swiftly turned to a potential fight with the champion Morrissey. Finally, a legitimate contender had emerged for Old Smoke's title. A showdown was inevitable.

Heenan began to chirp around town that he could handle Morrissey with ease in the ring. The champion, meanwhile, fired back with his own verbal attacks. The war of the words went on for some time until the Benicia Boy officially challenged Old Smoke for the championship by placing a card in the pages of the *New York Herald*. Morrissey accepted the challenge. The bout was the talk of the American sporting gentry and arguably the most important to date in the history of boxing.

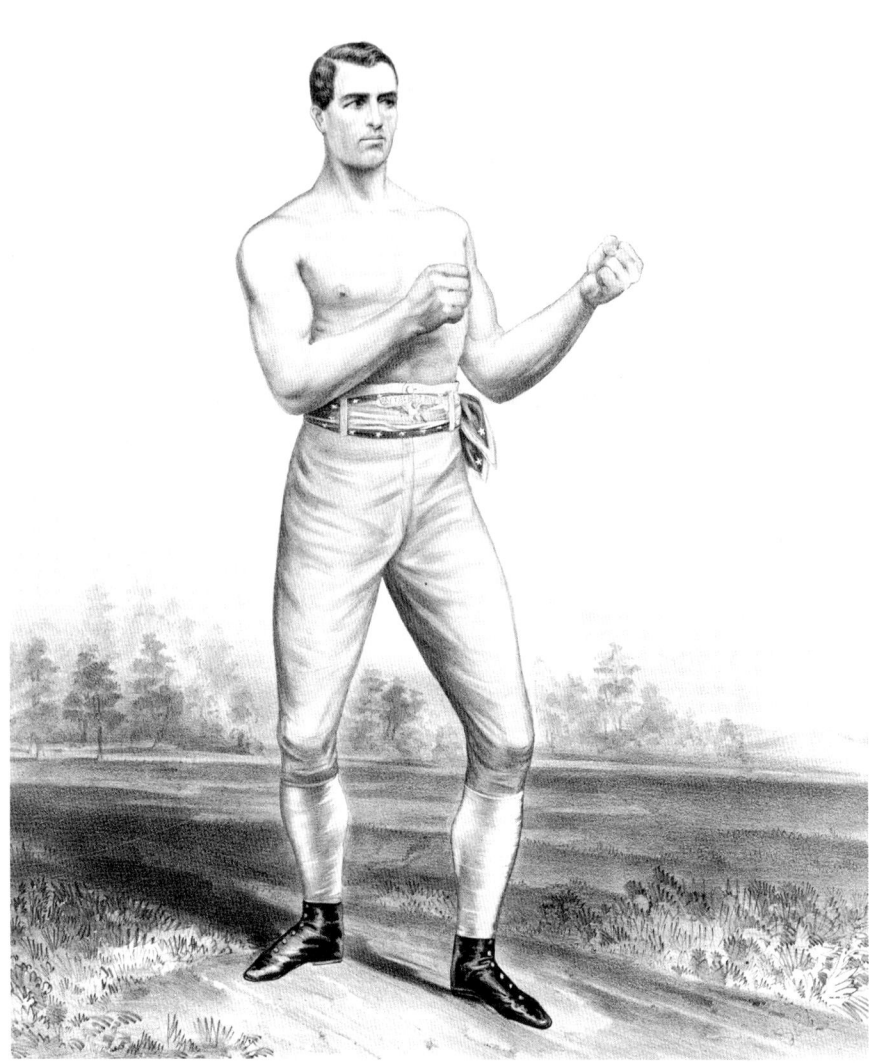

John Heenan, from a Currier and Ives print. *Library of Congress.*

Terms for the fight were agreed upon on July 19, 1858, in the offices of the *New York Clipper*. The sides had difficulty settling on particulars, but Morrissey won the coin flip to determine the fight's location and the other details were eventually settled. The fight would take place on October 20 with stakes of $2,500 a side. Morrissey immediately departed for Troy to train at the Abbey Hotel in the Lansingburgh neighborhood. Old Smoke turned to veteran trainer Jack "Shepherd" Hamilton to assist him in his conditioning.

Susie Morrissey pleaded with her husband to decline the fight, but Old Smoke wanted to prove he was a worthy champion. Heenan represented Morrissey's most difficult assignment to date, and Old Smoke relished the opportunity to let his fists fly once again. Even though he had a young son and Heenan was a dangerous foe, Morrissey did not adhere to his wife's wishes. He did, however, promise her, win or lose, the fight would be his last. A few days after agreeing to terms with Heenan, Morrissey's representatives chose Long Point Island on Lake Erie, about eighty miles from Buffalo, as the location for the fight. Having the bout on obscure and isolated Canadian territory reduced the potential for law enforcement to interfere with the proceedings.

With his fistic legacy at stake, Old Smoke concentrated solely on his training. The *New York Herald* sent a reporter to Morrissey's headquarters in Troy and reported the following:

> When we reached Morrissey's camp, the courteous and obliging "Shepherd" Hamilton informed us the Champion had not yet returned from his afternoon walk, having started with John Lawrence for a five-mile jaunt, but would be back shortly. In the meantime he invited us to make a tour of inspection.
>
> In the workshop a couple of pulleys, with thirty-six pounds attached to the strings, have been constructed, on which Morrissey works about an hour and a half each day. A sandbag is also suspended from the roof, on which he directs his blows with the naked fist. Three or four sets of dumbbells, of various sizes, are also freely used.
>
> His sleeping apartment is an immense room, extending the length of the house, with a current of air passing through—in it were about a dozen changes of garments, all clean as snowflakes. Everything about the place looked neat and tidy. After being shown everything appertaining to the training by his polite mentor, the blankets, the mask for sweating his face—which he has had on three or four times—we descended just in time to see John himself, accompanied by Lawrence, return from his journey. As the rubbing operation came off after every walk, an opportunity was afforded us of seeing personally the condition he is in, and we speak accordingly.
>
> All he had to do now is get the finishing touch, recruiting and hardening the muscles. His walking has been reduced from thirty-five or forty miles a day to twenty or twenty-four, which he performs with ease. He is in

splendid fettle, his broad shoulders, tapering waist, massive arms and upper works being supported by the strongest-looking pair of pins we ever saw. He has no superfluous flesh at all on any part of him.

He rises at five o'clock, partakes of sherry with eggs beaten in it, and starts for a five- or six-mile walk with his trainer before breakfast; on returning he proceeds to fight the bag, uses dumbbells and the pulleys with weights attached for about a half hour—change of clothes, rubbed down until the flesh is in a glow, and then to breakfast at eight o'clock, which consists of broiled chicken or mutton without any seasoning, a cup of tea and a slice of toasted bread. Half an hour's rest is allowed after breakfast, when a pleasant chat is had with his trainers and friends.

At half past eight o'clock, the usual morning walk of from eight to ten miles is gone over, and at half past eleven home again. Another half-hour exercise with the skipping rope, bells, weights, and bag, change of clothes and rubbed down—when dinner is announced. For this meal he is allowed beefsteak and currant bread, with a glass of sherry after it. Another resting spell is then allowed, and at one o'clock he starts off again for six or eight miles, varying the distance according as he feels, sometimes more and sometimes less, generally coming in again half past four. From this until six he has the gloves on with Mr. Lawrence, uses his bells, pulleys, skipping rope, and fights the bag, when he is again rubbed down and his clothes changed.

By this time supper is ready at precisely six o'clock, composed of broiled chicken, a cup of tea without sugar, and a slice of toasted bread, which he soaks well in the tea. Little or no water is allowed, or anything "slushy," as it would all have to be worked off again, and by avoiding them he saves himself much hard work. All his meals are prepared under Mr. Hamilton's personal supervision, and also served out by him—a regular quantity being allowed for each. No spices or seasoning of any kind are tolerated, but plain, substantial, and nourishing food. After supper he rows a boat for about four miles sometimes, however, taking a two- or three-mile walk, and winding up the day with a sprint race of a hundred yards at the top of his speed, which he accomplishes in a remarkably quick time, astonishing not only ordinaries, but also the professional "peds."

This completes his day's work, and, after being well rubbed down from head to foot, he retired at precisely nine o'clock to his virtuous pillow, to sleep like a top until five the next morning.

Various factions of the law looked to detain Morrissey and Heenan as they made their way to Long Point Island, but Old Smoke had several friends warn him of the tailing authorities. According to the *New York Clipper*, Morrissey also "made it a point of honor to keep Heenan as fully informed as he was himself of the danger of legalized disturbance." The championship belt, which had been presented to Old Smoke after he defeated Yankee Sullivan, "was left in charge of Mr. Riley, in Buffalo, subject to the order of the winner."

Although he was also diligent in his training, Heenan's appearance paled in comparison to the champion's. There were rumors that the Benicia Boy missed some conditioning time because of an ankle injury, but it did not appear to bother him once October 20 arrived. Morrissey's fanatical training regimen drew noteworthy praise in the newspapers. The *Clipper* reported: "On the day of the battle Morrissey was fine as a star, a perfect beauty, the embodiment of health, strength and endurance, and probably the best-trained man that ever entered the American prize-ring. For hours previous to the battle he was walking up and down the beach with his friends, and to all questions he gave the same answer—that he felt like a racehorse."

As was his nature, Old Smoke was the early aggressor when the fight commenced. Heenan, however, blocked Morrissey's early shots and caught the champion with a blistering right hand that opened up the skin under his left eye. The Benicia Boy had drawn first blood. Sensing an opportunity, Heenan immediately followed with three more quick hits that wobbled Old Smoke. Morrissey was able to grab the challenger and steady himself. The Benicia Boy broke the hold and gained an advantageous grip on the champ. He threw Morrissey down and began to taunt the champ's followers at ringside. Old Smoke's supporters were silent and stunned. John Heenan meant business.

Morrissey needed to find a way to counter the challenger's terrific power. He began to concentrate his blows on Heenan's ribs. Old Smoke relentlessly peppered the midsection, and the strategy began to pay dividends as the rounds progressed. Heenan's speed was gone, and Morrissey had little trouble targeting his opponent. Old Smoke effectively mixed body punches with rousing shots to the skull. The thousands in attendance—the majority of whom were in support of the champion—were most pleased.

By the end of the fifth round, Morrissey was in top form and Heenan was battered and weary. Old Smoke pitched his opponent to the ground to conclude the fifth, and the challenger needed the help of the men in his corner to get to his feet. Heenan was barely hanging on at this point, but he was a tough and determined warrior and would not go quietly. Morrissey continued to thump the challenger with vicious blows throughout the sixth,

BARE KNUCKLES & SARATOGA RACING

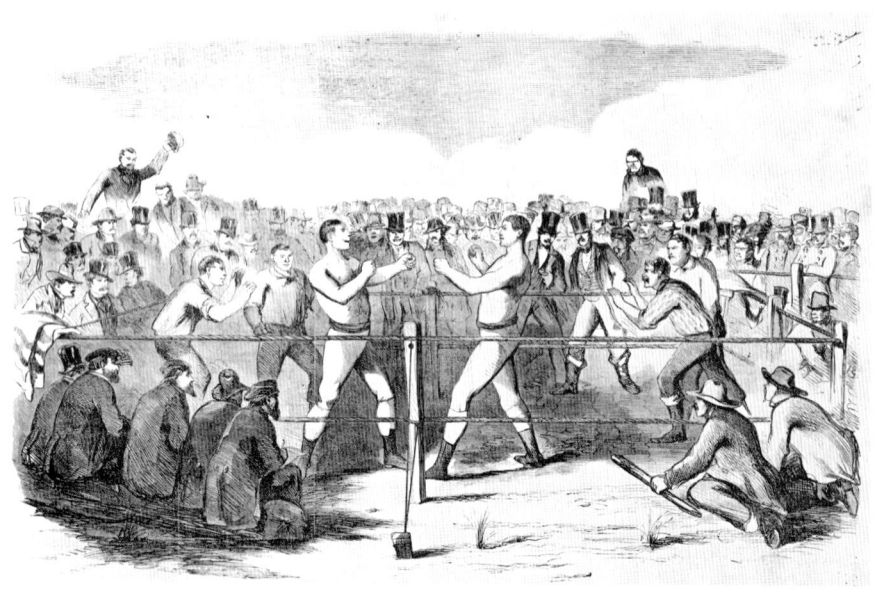

The championship fight between John Morrissey, *left*, and John Heenan, October 20, 1858. *From* Frank Leslie's Illustrated Newspaper.

seventh and eighth rounds. The Benicia Boy got a bit of a second wind in the ninth round and connected with a couple significant right hands to Old Smoke's jaw. Morrissey, however, seemed impervious to the hits. The champion pressed Heenan into a corner and knocked him to the dirt with a crackling left to the ribs.

The tenth round lasted only a few seconds. The challenger opened by swinging wildly and missing. Morrissey countered by unleashing a wicked right hand that caught Heenan square on the nose and sent him reeling to the ground. The Benicia Boy was once again in need of assistance to make it back to his corner. The end was near. Old Smoke had dominated his challenger, and now it was only a matter of completing the task and delivering a signature ending.

Heenan courageously came to scratch for the eleventh round, but it was obvious to all in attendance that he was licked. Morrissey approached his battered foe and fired a hellish right hand that broke the challenger's jaw—and his will. Old Smoke followed with a left hook to Heenan's neck. The Benicia Boy was done. His eyes closed, and he dropped to the ground. The fight was over. John Heenan had been knocked out, and Old Smoke had successfully—and conclusively—defended the American championship.

A LETTER FROM SARATOGA SPRINGS

John Morrissey promised his wife, regardless of the outcome, that his title defense against John Heenan would be the final time he would step in the ring. The Benicia Boy, his body and pride battered, was desperate to persuade Old Smoke to grant him another shot at the championship. There was tremendous public demand for a rematch, and the prize money figured to be substantial. Morrissey, however, intended to keep his word and resisted the temptation to throw down with Heenan a second time.

There were plenty of endeavors outside the ring for Old Smoke to attend to. He now had several gambling houses of his own and was a partner in numerous others throughout New York City. His duties in connection with Tammany Hall were rapidly expanding, and his political influence had grown to the point where the police never interfered in any of his activities. Still, there was great pressure for Morrissey to fight Heenan a second time. Old Smoke received frequent death threats for continuing to refuse to take up the challenge. He responded with an open letter in the *New York Tribune*:

> *Sir: Previous to my recent engagement with Mr. Heenan, I publicly announced that it would be my last fight. At its conclusion I proclaimed the same determination. Circumstances, seeming to me imperative, forced me into this contest. I considered myself obliged to make the match and fight it, determined by it to vindicate my honor and manhood, and to relieve myself from the persecution and assaults of my foes. I consider the first of these objects accomplished. No one has or can complain of the manner in which*

myself or my friends have conducted the fight. I had hopes that my second objective would also have been secured. I have no desire for further contest with any man. My duties to my family and myself require me to devote my time and efforts to purposes more laudable and advantageous. I hope to be permitted to do so without further interference from my late antagonist or his friends. I am aware of his published challenge and threat. It seems to be the determination to force me into another match, or assail me openly with violence. I now repeat that I shall never enter the prize-ring again, and those who know me will not misapprehend the motives for this resolution. It arises from no fear of any man, but from a desire to more fittingly discharge my duties to my family and society. Nor shall I be driven from this purpose by any threats of unlawful violence. I shall trust to the laws and the just influence of public sentiment to preserve me in the common privileges of an American citizen. If assaulted, I have no fear of my ability to defend myself, unless overcome, as I have been heretofore, by cowardly combinations. I shall exercise the right of defending myself, and trust to the countenance of all fair men to sustain me in my peaceable determination. Before the fight with Mr. Heenan, I declared publicly on the ground that if he vanquished me, I would take him by his hand and acknowledge my defeat without cherishing any animosity. My treatment of him and his friends after it was all over is well understood. It certainly was not illiberal or unkind. It is not for me to proclaim or boast of it, but I am entitled to say that it ought to protect me from all abuse from him or them.

JOHN MORRISSEY

While Morrissey's declaration did not totally squelch the matter, it did temporarily quiet the voices of Heenan and his cronies. Old Smoke, while still maintaining some ties to the streets, now spent much of his time meeting on equal terms with captains of industry and finance such as Cornelius "Commodore" Vanderbilt and Fernando Wood. He sought to distance himself from the likes of Dad Cunningham, Lew Baker, Awful Gardner and characters of that sort. Morrissey instead focused on spoiling his wife with beautiful gowns and sparkling jewels. They purchased a lavish home in New York City, and Old Smoke looked to leave his violent past behind.

Along with John Petrie, Morrissey partnered with the wealthy Matt Danser in a couple gambling houses. He had also ventured out on his own with an establishment at 8 Barclay Street. Old Smoke's Barclay Street house was elegantly furnished and catered only to the high rollers. Morrissey cleaned up with the place, earning more than $1 million during the next few years. Along

THE REMARKABLE LIFE OF JOHN MORRISSEY

with his ownership stake in the gambling houses, Old Smoke became an accomplished poker player, emptying the pockets of many men with his skill at card games. Morrissey was known to play poker in binges that could go days at a time. In one of these marathon sessions, he reportedly took $120,000 from Ben Wood, owner of the *Daily News* and Fernando Wood's brother.

Old Smoke continued to expand until he had stakes in at least sixteen gambling establishments throughout New York City. He took over the house at 5 West Twenty-fourth Street when owner Joe Hall lost all his money in bad investments and was forced to sell. It was the most popular gambling house in the city, and the money flowed to Morrissey. There were numerous anti-gambling factions, but none of these crusaders dared target Morrissey. The police would simply refuse to raid his houses. Old Smoke had all the right connections. His political clout was tremendous, and he had influential friends ranging from Wall Street heavyweights to feared killers in the Dead Rabbits. As his business interests flourished, Morrissey began to dabble in the stock market. He had become a favorite of shipping magnate Cornelius Vanderbilt and prospered from the Commodore's advice when it came to trading railroad stock. However, not all of the news was good for Morrissey. In March 1860, Old Smoke received word that his mother had died under mysterious circumstances. The *New York Times* reported from Troy:

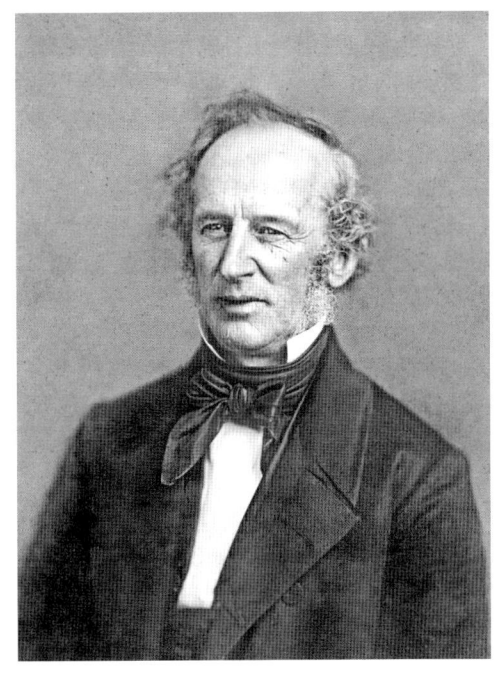

Commodore Cornelius Vanderbilt. *Library of Congress.*

> The body of Julia Morrissey, mother of John Morrissey, the known pugilist, was found yesterday morning about 6 o'clock, in the Poestenkill Creek, near the Second-street crossing. The body had the appearance of being in the water all night, and it is supported that in attempting to cross the Second-street bridge, she lost her way, walked into the creek and was

> drowned. Mrs. Morrissey was a woman of very unsteady habits, and has probably engrossed the attention of our police magistrates more than any other single person. She has repeatedly served terms in the penitentiary. During nearly a year past the unfortunate woman has been an inmate of the county home, which she left only a day or two ago, and has since been quite intoxicated. All efforts to reform her were beyond power. The inquest was held yesterday afternoon, and the jury brought in a verdict that Julia Morrissey came to her death by accidental drowning.

Julia Morrissey was fifty-four years old at the time of her death. Tim Morrissey, meanwhile, was living in a boardinghouse in Troy. Struggling with alcoholism and mental illness, he was a bitter man and had little contact with his family. The American dreams they once fought so hard for had long since been abandoned.

Although he maintained the stance that he was retired from the ring, there were always rumors that Morrissey was considering giving Heenan another opportunity. After much speculation—and more denials by Old Smoke—it appeared that Morrissey had changed his mind. In July 1860, the *New York Herald* printed a letter from Morrissey that he would indeed come out of retirement and fight John Heenan once again. The Benicia Boy had recently returned from England after fighting to a draw with British champion Tom Sayers. The *Herald* reported:

> As John C. Heenan has now arrived home, and he has, when in Europe, expressed so fervent a wish to fight me again, I will not balk him in his wish now I have him on the spot. I will fight him in four months from signing articles for from ten dollars to ten thousand dollars a side, and as it seems paradoxical to me and my friends to see a man dubbed champion of the world who has never won a fight in the ring, I will give him the chance he wants. I will meet him when and where he likes—put up what forfeit he likes—I to choose a stakeholder to be agreeable to us both. I trust outsiders will not interfere to prevent this match at—least until the money is up, which I am prepared to stake at drawing of articles.
>
> JOHN MORRISSEY

Heenan answered in the same publication two days later:

> I have noted with much satisfaction that John Morrissey declares that he will give me a second meeting in the ring. This in itself pays me for the

time I spent in England, and I at once accept all the terms he offers, and choose for stakes the highest sum he names. I will place in any responsible man's hands the sum of $2,500 for deposit for a match at $10,000 a side, pending the drawing of articles and selection of a stakeholder. I should have been pleased after my long stay abroad to have a few weeks of leisure to enjoy among my friends, but as there is no way in which I can be gratified so much as by being guaranteed an early match with Morrissey, I hope they will excuse me for this new occupation of my time. If Mr. Morrissey will send me word by note when and where he desires to see me for the arrangement of preliminaries I will meet him without delay, and the only further wish I now desire to state is that, like the stakes, the forfeit be large.

JOHN C. HEENAN

Morrissey, however, wrote to the *Herald* to debunk the authenticity of the initial challenge issued in his name.

Saratoga Springs,
June 17, 1860.

My attention has been called to a challenge purporting to come from me to John C. Heenan in your issue of this day. I desire to say in answer that I am not the author of this challenge, nor have I authorized any person or persons to issue such a challenge in my name. Moreover, I am not training for any fight, but am here for my health, and have business of more importance on hand than preparing for such a contest.

Yours respectfully,
JOHN MORRISSEY

It was never discovered who authored the original challenge in Morrissey's name. The champion intended to remain retired and did just that. He never fought Heenan, or anyone else, ever again. What was most interesting about Old Smoke's response in the *Herald* was the location from which it originated. The infamous John Morrissey had come to Saratoga Springs, New York. The sleepy village would never be the same.

Old Smoke likely knew of Saratoga during his youth, as the resort town was less than thirty miles north of where he grew up in Troy. Located on the southern end of the Adirondack Mountains, Saratoga already had a proud history by the time Morrissey began casing the place in the early 1860s. American soldiers earned a decisive victory over John Burgoyne and his British regiment near Saratoga during the Revolutionary War in the autumn of 1777. The crucial events at Saratoga led to America receiving assistance from France in the war effort against England. Many historians regard what took place in the two Battles of Saratoga as being among the most significant occurrences in the American struggle for independence. By the mid-1840s, the village had become a popular destination in the summer months for some of the wealthiest families in the country. The *New York Post* described Saratoga in its August 7, 1843 edition by publishing a letter from a vacationing gentleman:

> *I arrived here yesterday…a hot day…sandwiched like a boiled beef between several quiet old gentlemen, who had melted into butter, and as many unquiet young ladies.*
>
> *Saratoga, meaning both the hotels and the village, I found, of course, crammed with people. The United States Hotel is literally bursting, every chink and cranny being stuffed, and every door and window forming an outlet merely for the mass pent up within.*
>
> *It is said there are more than four thousand strangers in the place, among them Mr. Van Buren. He is proud and plump as a partridge in the fall…no less attractive to the eyes of the ladies than those of the politicians. Persons of less note are here in endless variety. Jonathan Goodhue and A.T. Stewart keep up the dignity of the New York millionaires.*
>
> *Coming down from Utica yesterday we were in the same train as John Quincy Adams. I was glad to see that he was cordially received wherever we stopped, for the old man, I think, has never received as much popular demonstration as his abilities deserve.*
>
> *At about three the carriages began to appear in front of the hotels, and the owners made up the cavalcade, which started on the afternoon drive, usually to Saratoga Lake. What a sight it was to see carriage after carriage start out, with splendid, high stepping horses, harness covered with silver and gold plated monograms; drivers with spotless liveries, tight knee breeches, high top boots and tall hats; carriages shining as if newly varnished. The ladies were costumed in the gayest of fashionable colors, with bright parasols.*

The rich and famous came for the healing waters and the spas. Prior to becoming president, George Washington traveled through Saratoga on horseback in July 1783 and made inquiries about purchasing the entire place. Celebrated writers James Fenimore Cooper, Washington Irving and

THE REMARKABLE LIFE OF JOHN MORRISSEY

Edgar Allan Poe later became regular visitors. It is even part of local lore that Poe composed a portion of "The Raven" in the woods near Revolutionary War hero Jacobus Barhyte's popular tavern. The railroad arrived in 1831, making the village more accessible, and several of America's grandest hotels—including the United States Hotel, Grand Union Hotel and Congress Hall—rose to national prominence. Those who came to Saratoga tended to fall in love with the place. John Morrissey was no exception. He also saw opportunity, envisioning a gambling and entertainment mecca, and profiting on the tourists during the warm summer months.

Setting the wheels in motion for the future, Old Smoke opened a gambling house in Saratoga on Matilda Street in 1861. Morrissey was generally welcomed in Saratoga. To keep in the good graces of the town fathers, he generously donated a significant amount of money to local schools, churches and hospitals. He also restricted locals from venturing into his Matilda Street house. Old Smoke believed it would be bad business to dip into the pockets of the Saratoga residents when there was plenty of money to be made from the wealthy vacationing set. His Matilda Street establishment operated at night during the summer season and was a successful venture. Morrissey, however, never rested on his laurels and looked for additional ways to profit in Saratoga.

Meanwhile, there was a war going on. In April 1861, Confederate forces fired on Fort Sumter in South Carolina, and the nation was suddenly tearing itself apart. During the next four years, more than 600,000 Americans were killed during the dark days of the Civil War. The fighting never reached New York City, but the war's impact almost destroyed the city nonetheless.

By July 1863, tensions in New York City had boiled over. As the Civil War was at the height of its carnage, the Draft Riots consumed New York. The culmination of working-class discontent with the new congressional laws to draft men to fight in the war, the riots forced President Abraham Lincoln to divert several regiments of militia and volunteer troops following the Battle of Gettysburg to New York in an attempt to restore order. The rioters were predominantly common laborers who were unable to pay a $300 commutation fee to spare themselves from service in a war many of them knew or cared nothing about. The rioting and looting lasted four days, and when the smoke finally cleared, the death toll was listed at 119. Homes, businesses, churches and even an orphanage were burned to the ground. Not all businesses were ransacked, however. Leonard Jerome, the "King of Wall Street," defended the offices of the *New York Times*, of which he was a major stakeholder, with a Gatling gun. Morrissey, meanwhile, enlisted

BARE KNUCKLES & SARATOGA RACING

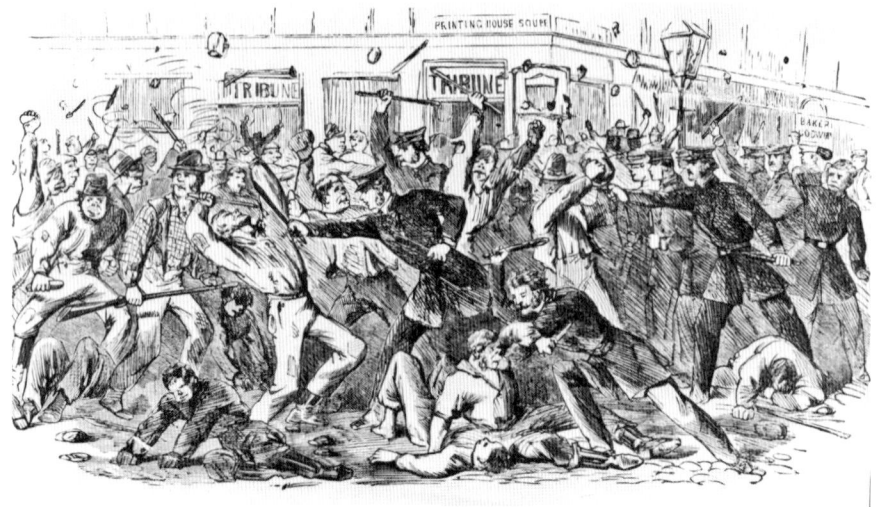

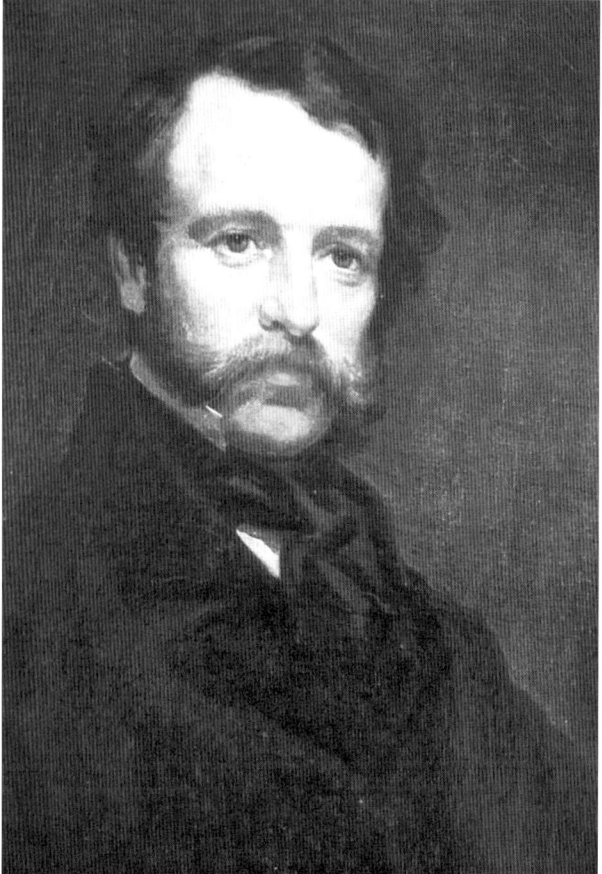

Above: New York City Draft Riots, 1863. *Library of Congress.*

Left: Leonard Jerome, one of the early leaders of Saratoga Race Course and builder of several tracks in the New York City area. *Courtesy of the National Museum of Racing and Hall of Fame.*

his old friends in the Dead Rabbits to protect his gambling houses without significant incident.

It was a peculiar time for Old Smoke to be conceiving a plan to bring thoroughbred racing to Saratoga Springs, but that's exactly what he was doing. Racing in New York had a checkered history and had been outlawed in the state for much of the first half of the nineteenth century. An 1802 law passed in New York read:

> *HORSE-RACING*
>
> An Act to prevent Horse-Racing, and for other purposes therein mentioned:
> *Passed March 19th, 1802*
>
> *Be it enacted by the People of the State of New York, represented in Senate and Assembly, that all racing and running, pacing and trotting of horses, mares or geldings, for any bet or stakes, in money, goods or chattels, or other valuable thing, shall be and hereby are declared to be common and public nuisances, and offences against this state; and the authors, bettors, stakers, stake-holders, parties, contrivers and abettors thereof, shall be proceeded against, and punished by fine or imprisonment at the discretion of any court having cognizance thereof; and all public officers concerned in the administration of justice are hereby strictly enjoined to cause this act to be faithfully executed.*

The law was unpopular from the beginning. A petition to the New York State Senate in 1804 stated that "the law against racing is so repugnant to the public sentiment that it is incapable of execution, and the unpunished violation of law has a tendency to bring into contempt the authority of government." But there were always people looking for loopholes in the law, and there were scattered reports of both running and trotting contests throughout New York during the ensuing years.

In 1821, Queens County was granted an exemption to the anti-racing law, but a similar request from Saratoga Springs was denied in 1825. George Cole and Alfonso Patten, a pair of Saratoga entrepreneurs, understood racing's popularity and took advantage of the ambiguity of the law by introducing trotting events under the guise that they were exhibitions of speed at the county fair.

With some financial assistance of a third party, the wealthy James Marvin, Cole and Patten built the Saratoga Trotting Course. On August 14, 1847, the immortal Lady Suffolk, known as "The Old Gray Mare" in Stephen

BARE KNUCKLES & SARATOGA RACING

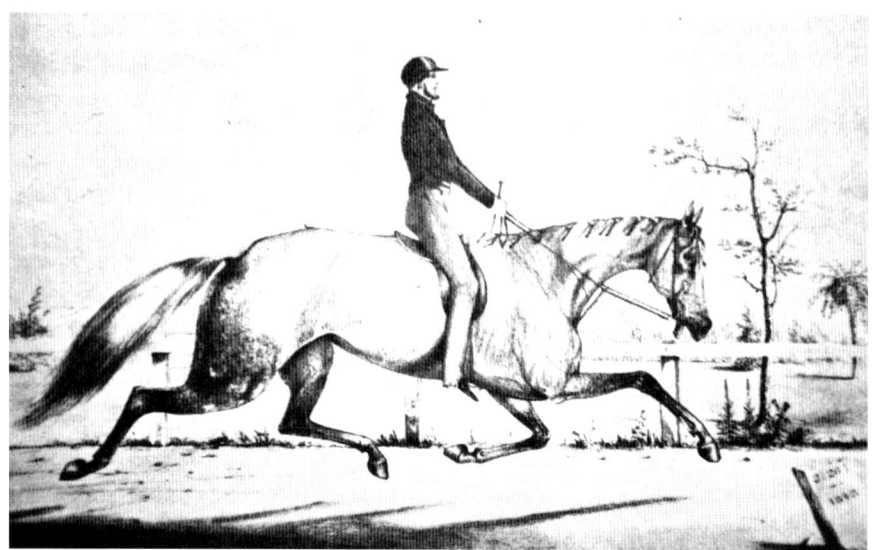

Lady Suffolk, one of the greatest trotters of all time and winner at Saratoga in 1847. *Library of Congress.*

Foster's folk song, opened the action at the new track with a sensational performance. Fourteen years old at the time, Lady Suffolk competed in what was supposed to be an exhibition to help promote the upcoming New York State Fair. The most famous horse in America, Lady Suffolk was a major drawing card, bringing an estimated crowd of five thousand to Saratoga. Lady Suffolk easily defeated Moscow in a best-of-five series of heats before the enthusiastic Saratoga gathering. The trotting meet featured four more days of racing, including a second match between Lady Suffolk and Moscow. The Old Gray Mare once again trounced her overmatched foe.

A month later, the state fair arrived at Saratoga. Five days of trotting events were a major part of the allure. Former presidents Martin Van Buren and John Tyler were in attendance, as was Millard Fillmore, who became president in 1850. A footnote in the reporting of the racing action confirmed the first thoroughbred race in Saratoga's history was also part of the festivities. On September 16, 1847, Lady Digby defeated Disowned and Hopeful in three straight heats in an event for "running horses."

Lady Suffolk returned to Saratoga in 1849 at the ripe old age of sixteen and was again victorious. She soldiered on to race with distinction through the age of twenty, compiling a record of ninety wins, fifty-six second-place finishes and only nine unplaced efforts in 163 official starts. The Old Gray Mare raced in seventeen states and was just as well known as John Morrissey later became. She was Saratoga's first sports hero—and Morrissey was determined to be its second.

Racing in Saratoga between 1847 and 1862 was sporadic. Several small tracks seemed to sprout up out of nowhere and were gone just as quickly, although the Saratoga Trotting Course remained and was used intermittently during this period. Then, in the summer of 1863, as America was engaged in war with itself, Old Smoke had a seemingly illogical idea of bringing organized thoroughbred racing into the mainstream. As was his self-assured nature, it was not unexpected that Morrissey made no pretenses of cloaking his vision under the ruse of a fair or "exhibitions of speed." Thanks to some obscure wording passed by the state on April 15, 1854, Old Smoke was able to execute a race meeting under the perceptible legal basis of "incorporation of associations for improving the breed of horses." He would get around to those pesky legal details of the actual incorporation in a couple years, but nobody seemed to object when advertisements in the *Daily Saratogian* from July 23 through July 27 announced Morrissey's undertaking. The ad stated:

> *Running Races! AT SARATOGA.*
> *Monday, Tuesday, Wednesday & Thursday*
> *AUGUST 3rd, 4th, 5th & 6th*
> *TWO RACES EACH DAY!*
> *Cards of Admission, $1.00*
> *For particulars, see Posters and Bills of each day. All sections of the North and West, and some portions of the South will be represented by their best horses, and Canada will also contend for some of the various purses. Excellent racing is anticipated.*
>
> *JOHN MORRISSEY,*
Proprietor.

Morrissey had beaten the bushes and was well prepared for Saratoga's inaugural thoroughbred meeting. Earlier in 1863, he had placed an ad in *Wilkes' Spirit of the Times* to recruit stable owners to support his vision. Old Smoke had originally planned three days of racing, but the response he received was so favorable that he was able to expand the program to include a fourth day. It was a remarkable achievement just to recruit enough stables to participate considering that organized thoroughbred racing had essentially gone dark throughout the country because of the war. The Union had requisitioned as many horses as it could for the war effort, and racing had even been interrupted in Kentucky, the epicenter of the sport. In fact, the track at Lexington was occupied for a time as Edmund Kirby Smith's Confederate troops camped on the dormant course in the months following the South's victory in the nearby Battle of Richmond.

But these troubles never reached Saratoga. Morrissey had convinced some of the most prominent racehorse owners in America—including Kentucky's John Clay, son of the famous politician Henry Clay—to bring their best steeds to compete on a trotting track in upstate New York. Old Smoke had once again gambled and bet on himself. It was another winning move.

On August 1, 1863, the *Daily Saratogian* reported, "String after string of the best racers in America have lately wended their way to the Springs, ridden by a man or boy in racing costume." That same day, the *Saratoga Republican* added, "The Race Horses at the Course will pass in review in front of the principal hotels this morning. The ladies will thus have an opportunity of seeing the noble animals who will contend for the various prizes next week."

In an exhibition of showmanship, the twenty-seven thoroughbreds expected to compete were paraded past the grand hotel piazzas along Broadway two days before the meeting was scheduled to open. The owners, horses, trainers, jockeys and stable workers came to Saratoga from all over. Fourteen stables, representing Kentucky, Missouri, Wisconsin, Illinois, Ohio, New York and Canada, were in town. Expectations were lofty. John Morrissey was about to preside over a historic spectacle and usher in a new era of elegance and sporting tradition in Saratoga.

THEY'RE OFF AT SARATOGA!

Sixteen years after the superb racer Lady Suffolk first brought tremendous crowds to the Saratoga Trotting Course, John Morrissey took the place to even greater heights. On Monday, August 3, 1863—one month after the Union army won two of the bloodiest battles of the Civil War at Gettysburg and Vicksburg—thundering hoofs were entertaining more than three thousand people at Saratoga Springs. Cards of admission were $1, and carriages surrounded the course to supplement the small capacity of the grandstand. On what the *Daily Saratogian* described as a "shimmering summer day," a dark bay filly named Lizzie W., with a one-eyed African American jockey in the irons, met the heralded colt Captain Moore in a best-of-three sweepstakes—$1,000 to the winner—to open the meeting. The *Spirit of the Times* commented that the track was "a mile out of town in a picturesque setting. The stables overlooked a rich, cultivated valley, many miles in width, to purple hills curtained with light summer haze far beyond."

There was an entry fee of $200 for the first race, and Morrissey added $300. Eight horses were entered, but six dropped out, with each owner paying $50 in forfeit, leaving Lizzie W. and Captain Moore to contest the opener. The signal for the first heat was given at 11:30 a.m. Billy Burgoyne, all ninety pounds of him, rode Captain Moore, while the jockey of Lizzie W. was described by the *Spirit of the Times* only as "the one-eyed black boy, Sewell." Captain Moore took the early lead along the rail before Lizzie W. earned a two-length advantage on the backstretch. Captain Moore recovered in the

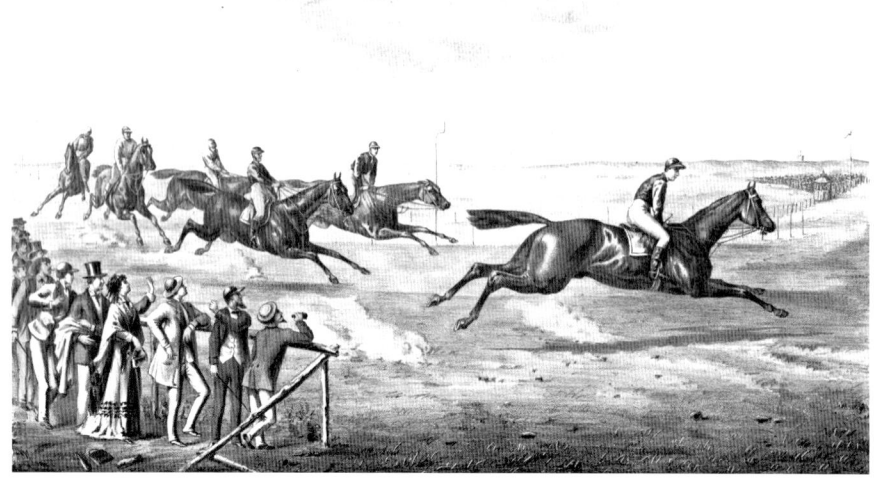

Saratoga Race Course scene from the 1860s. *Library of Congress.*

stretch, passed the filly and won the first heat. A twenty-minute rest period followed to allow the horses to cool off.

Sewell changed tactics in the second heat, allowing Captain Moore to take the lead along the backstretch. This time, Lizzie W. had plenty in reserve and collared her rival at the end to win by a neck. Sewell again held his charge back in the decisive heat, surrendering a four-length lead to Captain Moore. Lizzie W. displayed her closing kick again in the stretch and passed the colt with ease. Captain Moore began to sulk, and Lizzie W. won decisively to close out the contest.

The day's second event was a two-mile "dash" featuring the undefeated Thunder, a son of Lexington, as well as Jerome Edgar and the fillies Sympathy and Echo. Morrissey had recently purchased Jerome Edgar for $3,000 from John Clay and renamed the horse John B. Davidson in honor of a close friend. Morrissey's horse was the favorite and was ridden by famed jockey Gilbert Watson Patrick, better known as simply "Gilpatrick." Now in his mid-forties, Gilpatrick had received acclaim as the rider of great racehorses such as Boston and Lexington. He also went overseas with owner Richard Ten Broeck to ride Prioress, the first horse bred and owned by an American to win a significant race in England. Thunder set a torrid pace early on and was cooked by the end, while John B. Davidson dueled with Sympathy down the stretch. In the end, Morrissey's horse was defeated by a neck. The filly was owned by Dr. J.W. Weldon of Missouri. Weldon also owned Lizzie W., a full sister to Sympathy. A successful first day was in the books.

THE REMARKABLE LIFE OF JOHN MORRISSEY

Each of the four days of racing featured two contests that in several cases included multiple heats. An even bigger crowd, estimated at five thousand, attended the second day, which was highlighted by the favored five-year-old John Morgan winning a three-heat mile contest and the four-year-old mare Seven Oaks prevailing in a two-and-a-half-mile handicap with Sewell aboard. Henry Price McGrath, a friend and former gambling partner of Morrissey, was brought in from Kentucky to assign the weights in the handicap races. McGrath was so proficient at assigning weights that he created a constant fluctuation for favoritism in the odds among the trackside patrons in Dr. Robert Underwood's betting pools. McGrath later received fame as the breeder for Aristides, winner of the inaugural edition of the Kentucky Derby in 1875, and for founding McGrathiana Stud near Lexington, Kentucky.

Captain Moore got a shot at redemption on the meeting's third day in a best-of-five event at one mile. After defeating the filly Mammoma in the first heat, a powerful thunderstorm blackened the sky and delayed the proceedings. Once the storm passed, Captain Moore again bested Mammoma in the second heat and then dashed through the slop with Burgoyne aboard for an easy victory in the third to end the contest.

The final day of Morrissey's inaugural Saratoga meeting took place on Thursday, August 6, 1863, the same day President Lincoln declared a day of thanksgiving for recent Union victories. In Saratoga, that meant they celebrated at the track. Thousands were on hand. In the day's first contest, Sympathy defeated John Morgan in a pair of mile heats. Thunder was also supposed to be an entrant, but there was concern he had been drugged and the judges decided to scratch him. The meeting's closing race was another showcase for the superb Lizzie W., which won the finale at a mile and a quarter to give owner Weldon wins in four of the eight contests that summer.

The attendance for the four days was estimated at fifteen thousand. The cost of admission alone allowed Old Smoke to recoup the money put up for purses and turn a profit. Lizzie W. and Sympathy were the standouts among the thoroughbreds, winning twice each. Among the horsemen, the African American conditioner William Bird remarkably trained seven of the eight race winners. Bird would later receive acclaim for training Buchanan to victory in the 1884 Kentucky Derby.

Through sheer ambition and steely resolve, John Morrissey, at the age of thirty-two, had brought thoroughbred racing to the masses at Saratoga Springs. He had delivered another winner. The *Spirit of the Times* said Morrissey's meeting "laid the foundation for a great fashionable race meeting at the Springs" and

BARE KNUCKLES & SARATOGA RACING

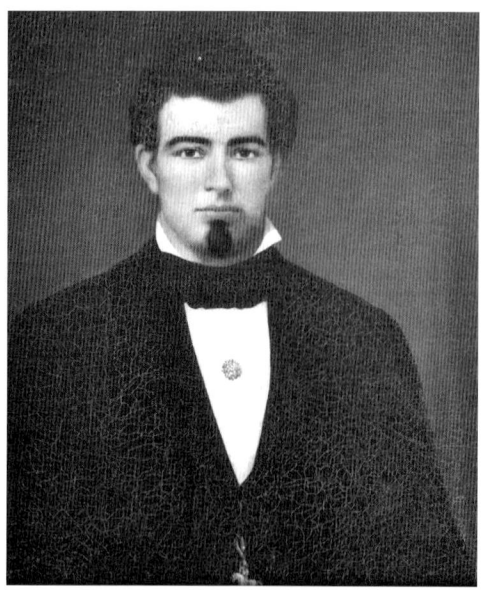

Painting of John Morrissey from his Saratoga Club House. The portrait remains on display there today as part of the collection of the Saratoga Springs History Museum. *Courtesy of the Saratoga Springs History Museum.*

added that "the formation of a competent club, and further proceedings, would seem to be a matter of course."

Although deemed a success, the inaugural Saratoga meeting was not without its criticisms. Much of the course was uneven, and sightlines were obscured in spots because of pine trees. The grandstand was insufficient, and the course had sharp turns and was almost three hundred yards short of its stated one-mile distance. Morrissey moved quickly to build on the meeting's success and address its shortcomings. To maximize the potential of his venture, Old Smoke acknowledged he needed the backing of respected sportsmen.

Although he had fame and wealth, Morrissey knew an undertaking such as the one he envisioned needed the endorsement of men with significant social standing to gain the acceptance of the upper crust of society that he was hoping to cater to. Old Smoke certainly had the connections. He enlisted William R. Travers, Leonard Jerome and John R. Hunter to front the operation. Commodore Vanderbilt also played a key role. While there was a faction of society that would not accept Morrissey because of his history of detaching people's eyes in street fights, there was no such issue with the men he brought in to share his Saratoga playground with.

Travers was a society wit and member of twenty-seven clubs in New York City. He was a wealthy broker and an aficionado of good wine and cigars. His *New York Times* obituary described him as "probably the most popular man in New York." Jerome, a lawyer, publisher and the grandfather of Winston Churchill, made a fortune on Wall Street and later played a major role in the opening of several racetracks, including Jerome Park, in the New York City area. He was also a partner with Vanderbilt in several of his railroad deals. Hunter was a respected owner and breeder of racehorses

THE REMARKABLE LIFE OF JOHN MORRISSEY

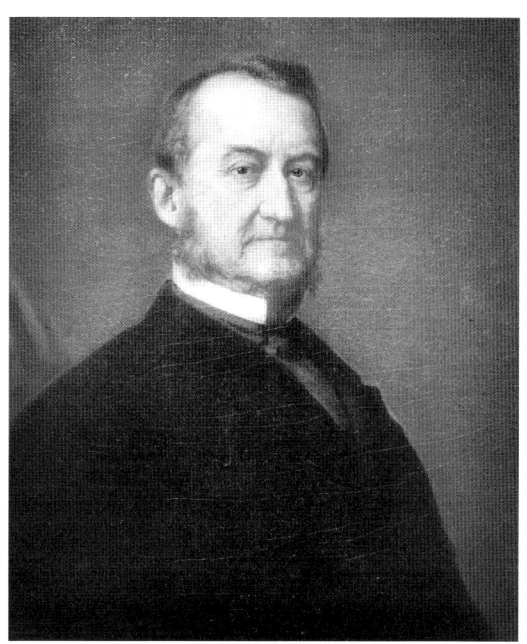

William Travers, first president of the Saratoga Association. *Courtesy of the National Museum of Racing and Hall of Fame.*

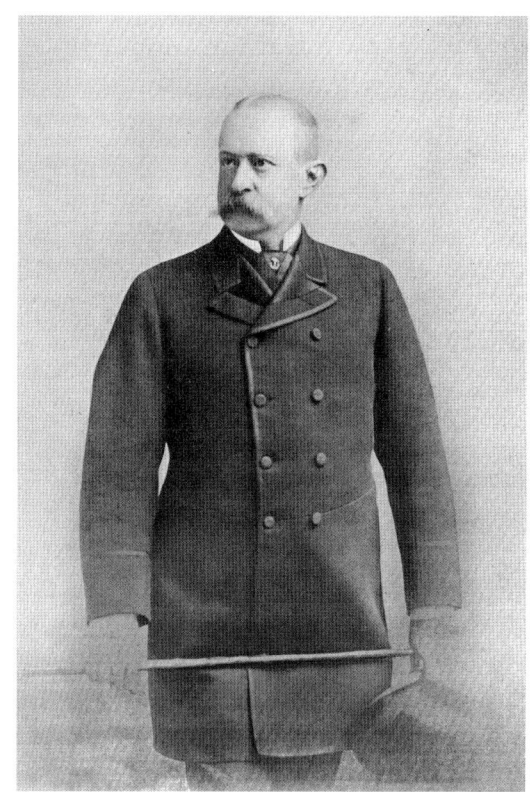

John R. Hunter, one of the early leaders of Saratoga Race Course and first chairman of the Jockey Club. *Keeneland Library.*

and partnered with Travers and George Osgood in Annieswood Stable. Hunter later became the first chairman of the Jockey Club and is credited with proposing the race that led to the creation of Pimlico Race Course in Baltimore, Maryland, home of the Preakness Stakes.

Travers was named the association's first president with Jerome as first vice-president and Hunter leading the executive committee. Others with key roles included John Purdy and Charles Wheatly. Purdy was a "gentlemen jockey," a term used for amateur riders of the era, and a wine dealer. He was named second vice-president. Wheatly arrived from Kentucky, where he ran the track at Lexington. He served as Saratoga's racing secretary and eventually became president of the Saratoga Association. Wheatly set most of the racing policy at Saratoga and also served as the track superintendent and clerk. He was one of the most respected men in racing and an excellent handicapper.

Also listed among the incorporators was James Marvin, who provided financial support to Cole and Patten back in 1847 for the Saratoga Trotting Course. A former state assemblyman, Marvin was serving as a United States congressman at the time and owned the massive United States Hotel in Saratoga. Others with roles included Osgood, a railroad executive and Cornelius Vanderbilt's son-in-law; John B. Davidson, a friend of Morrissey and a riverboat operator; Erastus Corning, president of the New York Central Railroad and a former congressman; Saratoga resident John White, a local government official; and John Eddy, a prominent Saratoga farmer.

Vanderbilt, by most accounts the wealthiest man in America at the time, stayed in the background, as did Morrissey—on paper, at least. Although they were from different walks of life, Vanderbilt and Morrissey were close friends. The Commodore greatly benefited from Old Smoke's influence in Tammany Hall when he began to consolidate his railroad empire. They openly socialized together in New York and even raced their trotting horses against each other throughout the city. Anita Leslie, the great-granddaughter of Leonard Jerome, noted that Morrissey, Vanderbilt and Jerome were regularly seen collectively in public. In *The Remarkable Mr. Jerome*, Leslie wrote:

> Since Jerome had entered as Vanderbilt's partner in the Harlem railroad, the three men were often seen together. Respectable citizens frowned….No one wanted to fall afoul of John Morrissey, or to delve too deeply into his affairs; they merely wished he would stay put in his sumptuous underworld casino and not be seen about. Well-bred folks disapproved, but could not resist watching as the suave intruder with the broken nose matched his horses in Harlem Lane against those of Vanderbilt, Jerome and Belmont.

THE REMARKABLE LIFE OF JOHN MORRISSEY

The only place Morrissey wasn't prominent was in the developing association's paperwork, which stated, "The objects of said association shall be to improve the breed of horses; and for carrying out the objects of this act, the association may hold one or more meetings upon their grounds each year."

Old Smoke's name was off the books, but he certainly wasn't silent in his partnership; he owned a controlling interest in the track and was in charge of all affairs relating to it. With Travers and the others serving as figureheads, it was time to move forward. The team Morrissey assembled was described in the *New York Herald* as "a guarantee of the thoroughly hightoned character of all the proceedings." The new association, although not yet officially incorporated, purchased 125 acres across from the Saratoga Trotting Course on Union Avenue for $100 an acre. It built a new mile course, erected a wondrous grandstand and spent freely to spruce up the land and offer the finest amenities.

By December 1863, the project was nearing completion, and Morrissey placed an ad in the *Spirit of the Times* announcing four days of racing at Saratoga in 1864. It was noted that the first race at the new course

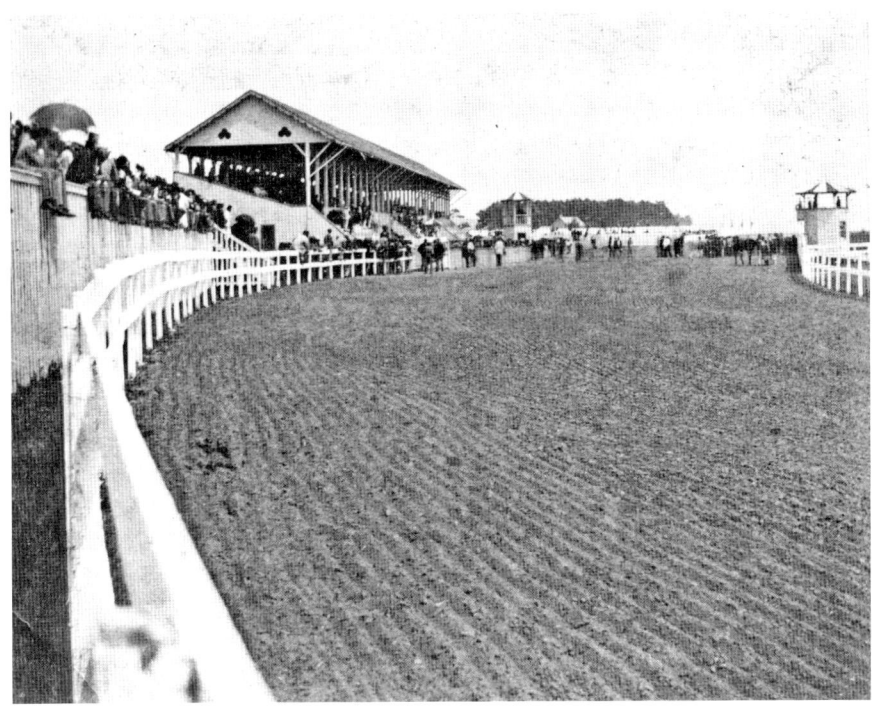

Saratoga Race Course, 1867. *Courtesy of the National Museum of Racing and Hall of Fame.*

would be the Travers Stakes for three-year-olds. The entry fee was set at fifty dollars.

The Civil War raged on in the South through the following spring and summer as the finishing touches were being completed on the new Saratoga Race Course. The Union army was closing in on a key victory at Petersburg, Virginia, when the grand venue opened for the first time on August 2, 1864. Named in honor of the association's president, the Travers Stakes was the first race carded at the new facility. Travers, Hunter and Osgood entered their mighty colt Kentucky. He became the star of the show.

Arguably the greatest racehorse of the Civil War era, Kentucky was a son of the immortal Lexington, sixteen times America's leading sire. Kentucky lost his first race as a three-year-old in 1864, but he rounded into top form during his victory in the two-mile Sequel Stakes at Paterson, New Jersey, prior to his arrival at Saratoga. The Travers, run at one and three-quarter miles, featured a five-horse field competing for a purse of $2,500. The talented colt Tipperary, which finished ahead of Kentucky during the latter's lone defeat in the Jersey Derby, was a slight favorite among the bettors. With an

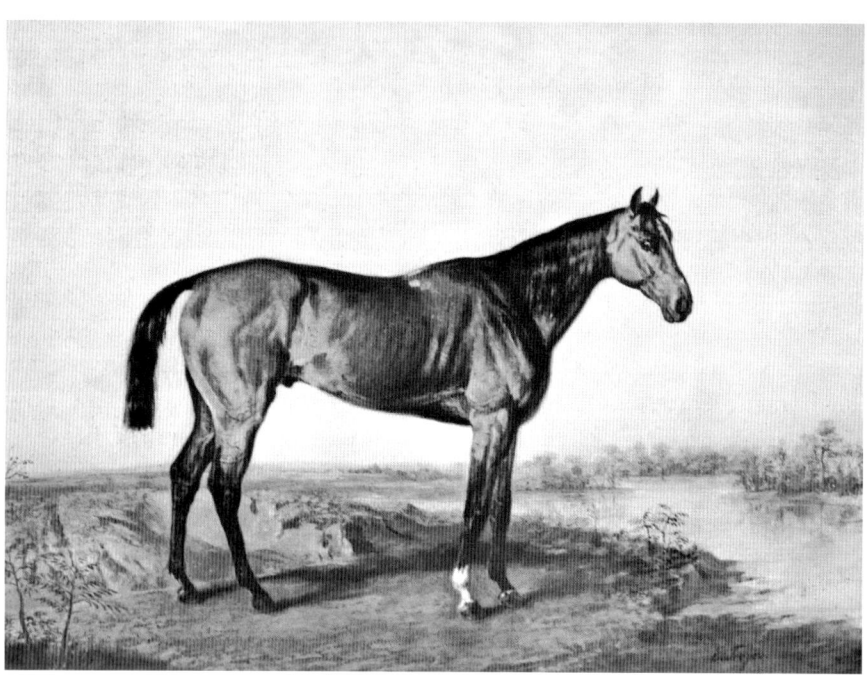

Kentucky, winner of the inaugural Travers Stakes and the first two editions of the Saratoga Cup, from an Edward Troye painting. *Courtesy of the National Museum of Racing and Hall of Fame.*

estimated crowd of five thousand on hand, Kentucky displayed his brilliance with an easy three-length victory over Tipperary, gloriously cantering home in the stretch as Gilpatrick geared him down.

Two days later, Kentucky and Tipperary met again at Saratoga in a two-mile contest worth $1,750. Carrying five more pounds than his rivals as a result of his Travers victory, Kentucky also had to deal with Orion and Patti in addition to Tipperary. He made easy work of them all and won by three lengths to confirm his status as the best horse in the land. Tipperary, again second to Kentucky, did get a consolation prize with a victory the following day. After three grueling races in four days, Tipperary was wiped out and never raced again.

Kentucky, meanwhile, never lost again. Following his two wins at Saratoga that summer, he won seventeen more in succession throughout the next two years, including the 1865 and 1866 editions of the prestigious Saratoga Cup, to cement his status as Saratoga Race Course's first equine sensation. By the time he was retired, Kentucky had won twenty in a row and had only one defeat on his ledger of twenty-one starts. He was eventually immortalized with a rightful spot in the National Museum of Racing and Hall of Fame.

As was the case in 1863, the first meeting at the new Saratoga Race Course in 1864 was expected to feature four days of racing. However, as it was such an overwhelming success, a fifth day of racing was added to the schedule. On that day—Saturday, August 6—the track played host to its first steeplechase event. A prominent fixture in Canada, few of these races had ever been seen in America. The two-mile race featured four hurdles per mile and was won by Garryowen. The crowd of more than six thousand was entranced by seeing "five horses leap hurdles 3½ feet high, with well-grown men on their backs," according to the *Daily Saratogian*.

All of the problems Morrissey encountered the year before—the inadequate grandstand, uneven track, poor sightlines, etc.—had been addressed at the new plant. The new grandstand, two hundred feet long with a seating capacity of two thousand, was described in the *Daily Saratogian* as "a model of elegance." At the close of the 1864 meeting, the *New York Times* remarked that Saratoga "will henceforth be regarded as the best race course in the country."

The racing association was officially incorporated under New York law on March 21, 1865, as the "Saratoga Association for the Improvement of the Breed of Horses." A couple weeks later, on April 9, Robert E. Lee, commander of the depleted Confederate army, surrendered to Ulysses S. Grant at Appomattox Courthouse in Virginia to officially end the Civil War.

BARE KNUCKLES & SARATOGA RACING

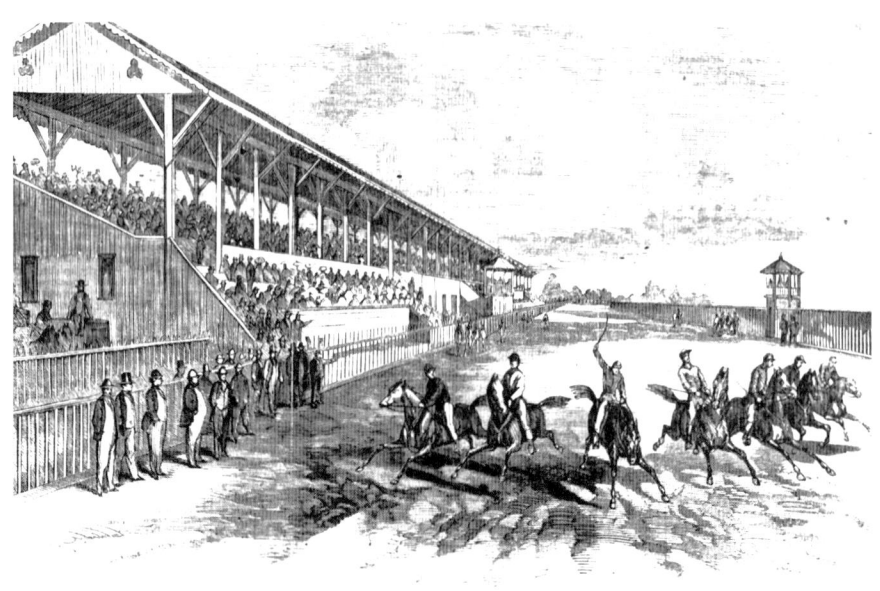

Saratoga Race Course, 1870s. *Courtesy of the National Museum of Racing and Hall of Fame.*

Saratoga's popularity continued to grow that summer. The track handled its biggest crowd yet—numbering an estimated ten thousand—in August 1865, when the legendary Kentucky returned to win the Saratoga Cup. The *New York Times* provided a glowing report of the action at Saratoga that summer:

> The concourse of spectators present is estimated by thousands. The grand stand was full to overflowing with fashionably dressed ladies and children, and well-behaved and well-dressed men. The field stand was also well filled; a dense crowd filled the space between the stands, and on either side to the right and left. There never was a better behaved assemblage on a race-course or elsewhere than was assembled here to-day. During the whole time nothing occurred to mar the pleasures of the occasion. If the 2,000 thieves, roughs and blacklegs reported to have arrived were there, they were on their good behavior, and did not make themselves known; if there were any plug-uglies present, they made themselves known only to the initiated. A wonderful occasion indeed—not an intoxicated individual to be seen; there was no loud talking, no vulgar expressions made use of, no immoderate manifestations of disapprobation or approbation; not a pocket was picked, or a man knocked down, so far as could be ascertained. Whole family parties—composed of the most respectable citizens—were seated

in groups upon the main stand, and had the pleasure of witnessing one of the best races in—many respects that—ever came off in this country, without hearing a word to offend the most sensitive ear. On the quarter in front of the main stand loomed up the muscular form of John Morrissey, surrounded by the members of the Track Association, the owners of horses entered and, others who wished to bet upon the result of the contest. So orderly an assemblage never was seen before on any other track in this country. Whoever heard of such a race-track scene in this country before? The unanimous voice among the knowing ones is that John Morrissey deserves the honor.

With his track a resounding success, Morrissey enjoyed the spotlight with his wife. At the track and in town, people regularly asked where they could spot the beautiful and refined Mrs. Morrissey, who was always in the latest fashions. Old Smoke, meanwhile, regularly wore a tall hat, swallow-tailed coat, striped trousers and patent leather boots. He sported a $5,000 diamond on his shirt and smaller diamonds in his cuff links. He had come a long way since his days of cracking heads along the Troy docks. Even President Lincoln spoke of Morrissey. In a biography by Carl Sandburg, the president compared one of his indecisive generals to a former Tammany Hall subordinate of Old Smoke. As Lincoln told the story, on learning a fellow Tammany man was getting married, the Morrissey minion looked jittery and asked the bridegroom, "Have you asked Morrissey yet?" Lincoln added: "This general…wouldn't dare order the guard out without asking Morrissey."

Saratoga Race Course continued to prosper under Old Smoke's leadership. The crowds and the purses grew steadily, and the quality of racing was widely considered the best in America. Throughout its first decade, Saratoga's famous oval attracted greats such as Parole, Ruthless, Harry Bassett and Longfellow. The likes of Duke of Magenta, Miss Woodford, Hindoo, Emperor of Norfolk and Luke Blackburn soon followed. The great riders, including Gilpatrick, James McLaughlin, Isaac Murphy, George Barbee and Lloyd Hughes, were all Saratoga regulars in the early days. Although trainers didn't get much notoriety in the newspapers of the era, Saratoga also featured the best of that profession. Ansel Williamson, R.W. Walden, Edward Brown, William Burch and Jacob Pincus were all based at Saratoga in the summer. Each of the aforementioned horses, jockeys and trainers was eventually recognized as a luminary of the sport and enshrined in the Hall of Fame.

BARE KNUCKLES & SARATOGA RACING

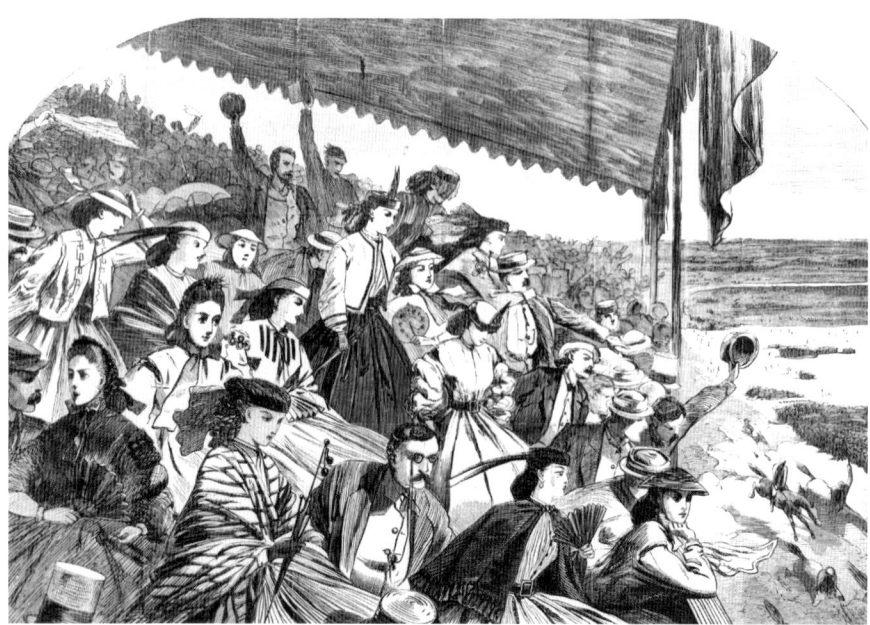

Winslow Homer's rendition of Saratoga Race Course in the mid-1860s. *Courtesy of the National Museum of Racing and Hall of Fame.*

Although there was considerable talent on the track, some of the racegoers at Saratoga were even more distinguished. It was not uncommon to see the likes of famous Civil War generals such as Ulysses S. Grant, William Tecumseh Sherman and Philip Sheridan holding court at the Saratoga races. They were all known to socialize with the grand impresario himself, John Morrissey, who had become so well versed in all matters of the turf that he was often seen personally training and caring for the horses in his own stable.

Old Smoke was perpetually pondering his next big move, but where could he go from here? With his track and its product both proving to be exceptional and his numerous gambling houses bustling with activity, what could possibly be on the horizon that would satisfy Morrissey's restless nature? Many people would have been content, but remaining idle was never John Morrissey's style.

THE HONORABLE JOHN MORRISSEY

In the mid-1860s, with Saratoga Race Course flourishing and his gambling houses churning out a steady profit, John Morrissey began to shift much of his attention to the political arena. The concept of a former bare-knuckle pugilist and notorious gambler becoming a United States congressman was of course completely nonsensical, but Old Smoke had already established a considerable record of defying the odds. For years, in a variety of roles ranging from enforcer to trusted consultant, Morrissey had been an important cog in the Tammany Hall political machine. With his national fame—he was described as "known the country over" by the *New York Times*—and the backing of Tammany, Old Smoke was plotting a move up the political food chain.

Along with the tremendous clout of Tammany Hall, Morrissey had an additional heavyweight in his corner. The wealthy and influential Commodore Vanderbilt became one of Old Smoke's biggest advocates. In addition to their shared love of horses and gambling, Old Smoke and the Commodore had a history of political and financial dealings. As he built the Harlem Railroad, Vanderbilt relied on Morrissey's political weight to help grease the wheels of the project with minimal interference from opposing interests. In turn, the Commodore helped sponsor Old Smoke's racetrack with both capital and the recruitment of other men of prestige. While he wasn't a traditional politician or a slick orator, Morrissey was well versed on the ins and outs of the political game and desired to be on the playing field.

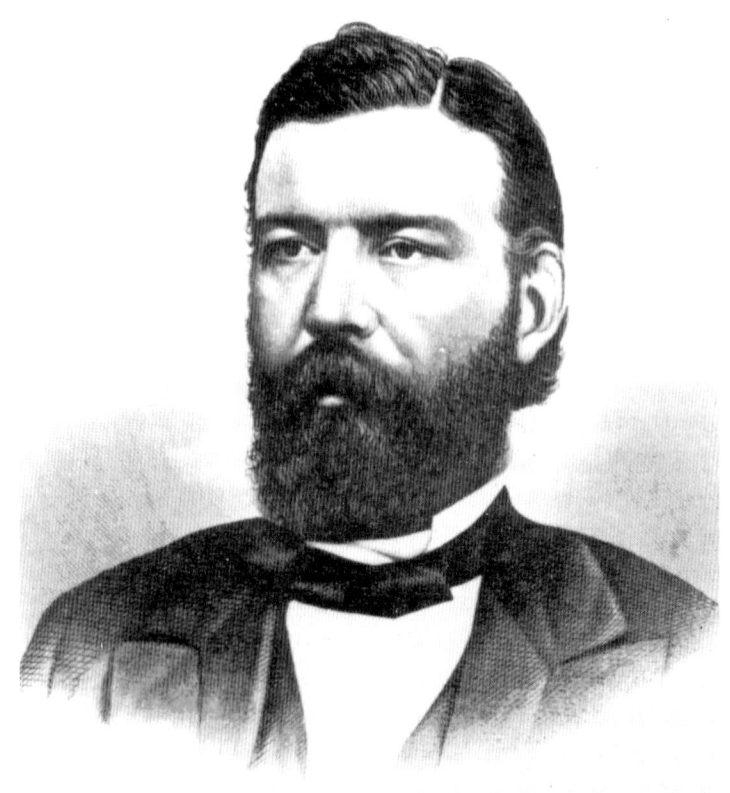

John Morrissey, United States congressman. *Courtesy of the National Museum of Racing and Hall of Fame.*

THE REMARKABLE LIFE OF JOHN MORRISSEY

William M. "Boss" Tweed, the corrupt leader of Tammany Hall. *Library of Congress.*

William Magear "Boss" Tweed had ascended to the top of the Tammany Hall pecking order as the organization's "grand sachem." For years, Morrissey was a loyal Tammany man and Tweed supporter, but Old Smoke had grown tired of the unethical and illegal dealings of the Tweed Ring. During his run as Tammany's ruler, Tweed and his cronies built arguably the most corrupt and larcenous political machine in United States history. The Tammany thieves robbed, by some estimates, as much as $200 million from New York City's coffers. The Tweed Ring was as organized as it was shameless. Tammany controlled the legislature, courts, treasury and ballot box. Tweed had judges, cops and journalists on his payroll. He stole at will, laundered the money and had his fingers in essentially every cake in the city.

Tweed was smart in recognizing that he didn't want John Morrissey as an enemy. Old Smoke had the necessary support to be a major nemesis to Tammany if he elected to go that route. Tweed did all he could to placate Morrissey, pledging Tammany's endorsement and resources in a bid for the United States House of Representatives. With the backing of Tammany Hall, and his own considerable popularity, John Morrissey was elected to Congress in 1866 as a representative of New York's Fifth District. For the time being, at least, the thought was that this would keep Old Smoke from badgering Tweed and his business of stealing everything he could. Morrissey's election predictably created quite a stir in the papers. All the way out in Wisconsin, the LaCrosse *Democrat* reported:

Who and what is Morrissey?

He is a stout, good-looking Irishman. He weighs about one hundred and eighty-five pounds. He has a good head, a clean brain, a deep, earnest, fearless brown-black eye; he speaks slowly and earnestly; he is about five feet eleven inches high, broad shouldered, deep chested, strong of muscle; his hair is a beautiful glossy black, slightly wavy, worn reasonably long, and flecked with a few gray sentinels; his beard and mustaches are worn full; he dresses in faultless black broad-cloth, wears a single diamond bosom pin, worth five thousand dollars, a large signet ring, and sleeve-buttons studded with diamonds; he is wealthy; he is liberal to the poor, giving thousands of dollars yearly to objects of charity; he pays a hundred cents on the dollar for all he owes; he champions the poor and defenseless; he moves in the best society in New York; he is a clear-headed business man, with broad, liberal national views.

He was a poor, ignorant boy; brought up much as are preachers' sons, to all manner of devilment, and a credit to nobody. He has risen from the lowest rounds—he came from the lowest walks of life, through ignorance and bad education, to the position he occupies.

John Morrissey is a gentleman who minds his own business, and is a thousand times more respectable than nine-tenths of the ministers of the gospel of this country or their ranting followers…Morrissey talks, acts, appears like a gentleman of sense.

He had a prize match with Heenan once, but when the contest was over, he shook hands with his opponent. The example of Morrissey would be a good one for Radicals to follow…He is more honest, more liberal, more trustworthy, more patriotic, and has a better record every way than half of the Republicans, and the pluck to meet his enemies in a fair, square, stand-up fight.

All eyes were on Morrissey when he arrived in Washington. In March 1867, the *New York Times* stated:

Of all the members of the new Congress, Mr. Morrissey, of this City, appears to attract the most interest in Washington. We are told that when he made his appearance to be sworn in on Monday, the anxiety of the House and the galleries to get a glimpse of him was intense. The telegraph, with some confusion of language, says that "his fine personnel astonished many who had formed their opinions of him, based upon ideas obtained by the popular conception of his character." Members crowded round his seat to congratulate him, and the brilliant array of ladies who on this occasion were scattered all over the House, gave evidence of something more than curiosity concerning him. The first public act of Mr. Morrissey after being sworn in was to enter his protest, in company with his fellow Democrats, against the exclusion of Southern representatives from their seats in Congress, and the protest received emphasis from the fact that he joined in it.

If, now, Mr. Morrissey chooses to take advantage of his opportunity in Congress, he can make a mark which few of his fellow members have the chance to do. And in this we must not be understood as saying anything funny, or with a double meaning. Any one might envy him the chance of fame that lies in his first speech. We venture to say that no orator ever stood in Congress with more eager listeners than he will when he opens his mouth to deliver his maiden speech; and no speech was ever perused with more interest by the country than his will be when he gives the opportunity. If he takes up, as we have no doubt he will, the question of reconstruction; and if he delivers an oration worthy of the theme and the hour, he may not only aid in bringing order out of political confusion, but he may raise a monument to his own name more durable than that of which Virgil sings…Let him, at the same time, with patriotic independence, spurn the Copperhead counsels of Brooks and Fernando Wood, and he will soon be able to justify the interest which his presence has already excited in Washington.

Ultimately, there was little of substance Morrissey was able to accomplish once in the House. The South had been devastated by the Civil War, and the nation's finances were in shambles. Old Smoke was unable to offer much help on agrarian issues or the complex economic problems that hampered the country, but he still earned respect as a practical politician. Morrissey also showed his polarity while in Washington.

Demonstrating his compassion, Old Smoke was one of only four Democrats who supported a bill awarding Mrs. Lincoln a pension following the president's assassination. Demonstrating he was also still a man not to be trifled with, he once famously bellowed from the floor of Congress during debate that "if any gentleman on the other side wants his constitution amended, just let him step into the rotunda with me." Not surprisingly, there were no takers.

Although he rarely voted and was absent much of the time while tending to other interests, Morrissey's first term in Congress was praised by Tammany Hall, and he was subsequently reelected. Throughout his time in Congress, Old Smoke maintained his presence in Saratoga Springs and continued

BARE KNUCKLES & SARATOGA RACING

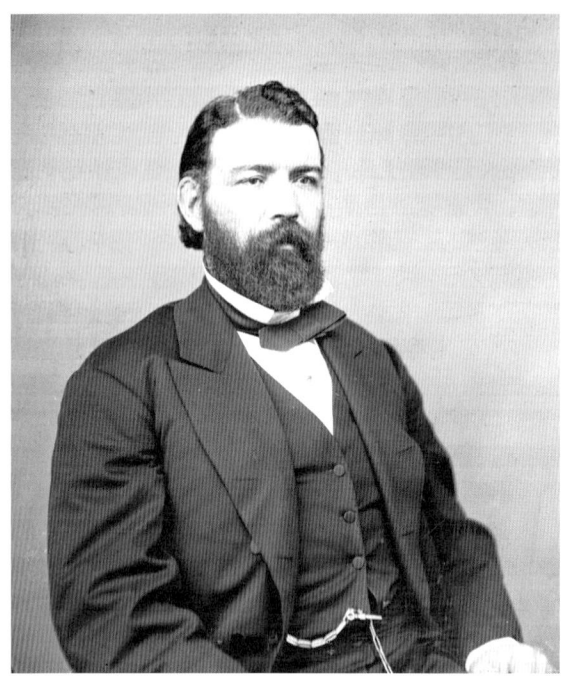

Left: John Morrissey served two terms as a United States congressman and was later elected twice to the New York State Senate. *Library of Congress.*

Below: John Morrissey's Club House in Congress Park, Saratoga Springs, New York. *George S. Bolster Collection of the Saratoga Springs History Museum.*

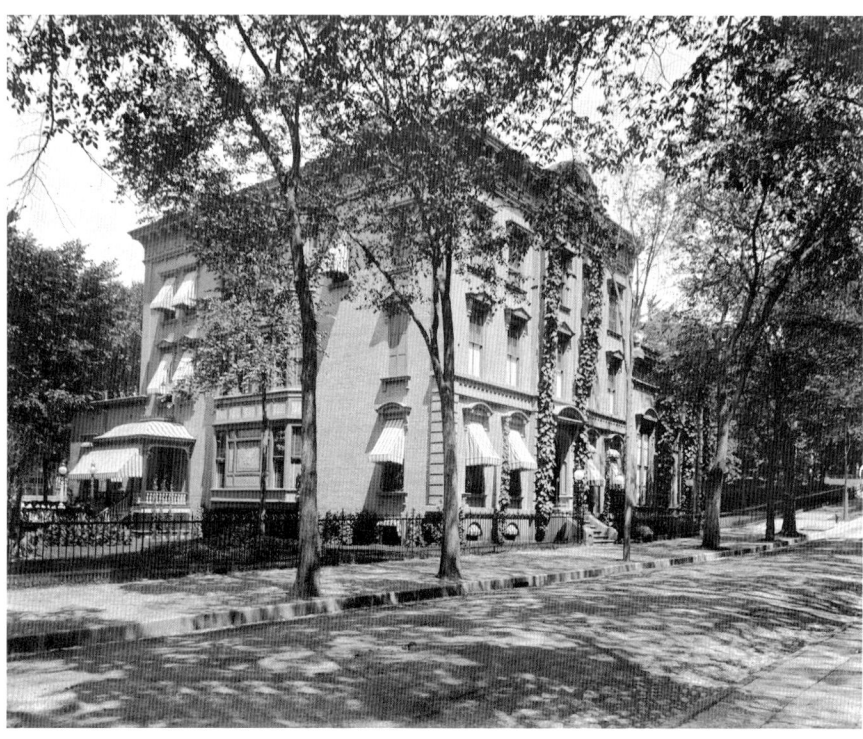

the practices that led Saratoga Race Course to become America's finest racetrack and one of the world's most revered sporting venues. As Saratoga continued to grow—both the track and the village—Morrissey advanced on yet another opportunity. His Matilda Street gambling house was always profitable, but the venue was small in comparison to his New York City establishments. Saratoga had America's greatest sports facility and some of the country's finest hotels and spas. Now it was only a matter of time before the visionary Old Smoke unveiled the next big thing.

Morrissey chose Congress Park in the heart of the village for his grand Club House. Construction began in 1867, and no expense was spared. Old Smoke shelled out hundreds of thousands of dollars, including an initial investment of $190,000. The dining room featured a $60,000 chandelier and a $40,000 rug imported from Scotland. Exquisite French chairs and mirrors fifteen feet tall with elaborate carved frames were installed. A massive steel safe, six feet by eight feet with four combinations, was located in Morrissey's office. A large portrait of the proprietor, inscribed, "Honorable John Morrissey, member of Congress," hung above the fireplace.

The Club House opened for business in 1870—and business was good. Hailed as an architectural masterpiece, the three-story brick structure featured games of roulette, poker and faro, among others. The games were of the highest stakes and drew some of the most prominent and wealthiest individuals in the country. President Ulysses S. Grant and future presidents Rutherford B. Hayes and Chester A. Arthur were patrons in the early years. Commodore Vanderbilt, John Rockefeller and Jay Gould were regulars. Even a young writer named Samuel Clemens stopped by on occasion. He, of course, was much better known by his pen name, Mark Twain. The house served caviar, quail, the finest wines and expensive cigars.

With his grand facility featuring lavish furnishings and the finest food and drink, Morrissey also made it a priority to hire the best staff money could buy to oversee the table games. He lured the famous faro dealer Hamilton Baker to the Club House for a salary of $4,500 per month. Baker was in such great demand that he also received a cut of the house profits, and in some years his earnings surpassed $70,000. It was all money well spent. The Club House was a national draw from the beginning and was netting an annual profit of $500,000 by 1872. Saratoga, thanks in large part to Old Smoke's efforts at the track and the Club House, became one of the premier resort destinations in the world.

Not everyone was welcome, however. From the start, Morrissey banned women from the gambling rooms. They were allowed in the Club House's

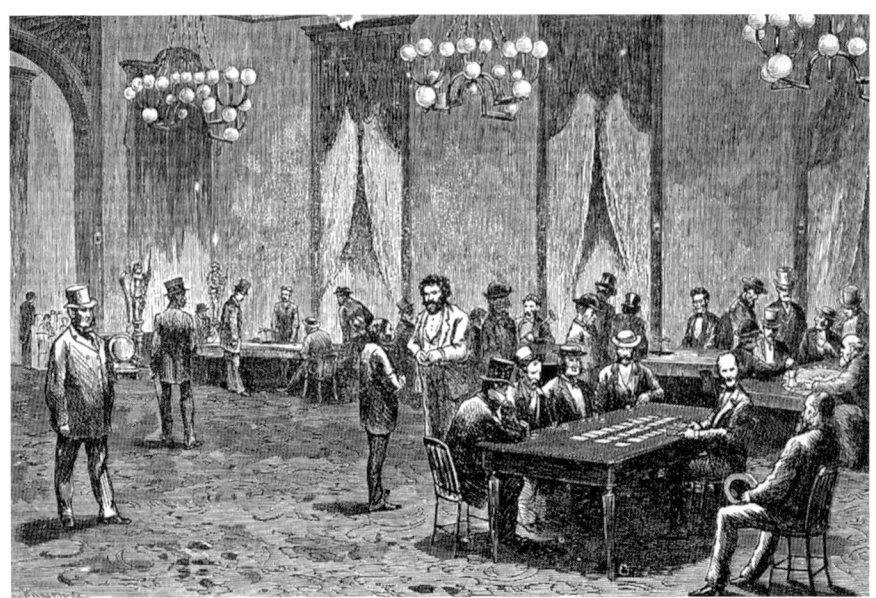

The imposing John Morrissey in one of the gambling rooms at his Club House in Saratoga Springs. *Courtesy of a private collection.*

drawing rooms, but the tables were exclusively for the men—as long as they weren't from Saratoga Springs. Maintaining the policy he had at his Matilda Street facility, Old Smoke was adamant that no local residents were to be permitted to gamble in the Club House. Morrissey wanted to remain in the good graces of the village leaders who insisted he avoid profiting from the locals. To ensure he had continued support of the local politicians, Old Smoke continued to donate generously to charities and civic causes. If Saratoga needed anything, Morrissey provided it. Old Smoke was regularly seen greeting his Club House guests in Congress Park. Typically wearing white gloves to cover his scarred and misshapen fists and carrying a green umbrella rain or shine, the legendary gambler was even known to deal cards from time to time for his highest rollers.

Saratoga Race Course and the Club House enjoyed a symbiotic and profitable relationship under Old Smoke's direction. The track was averaging more than ten thousand in daily attendance during the early 1870s, and betting at the track and through pool selling at the Club House was brisk. Morrissey, of course, controlled the pool sales, an important source of his income. He regularly auctioned the pools at the Club House himself with the sales starting early in the morning in a betting room adjoining the main

THE REMARKABLE LIFE OF JOHN MORRISSEY

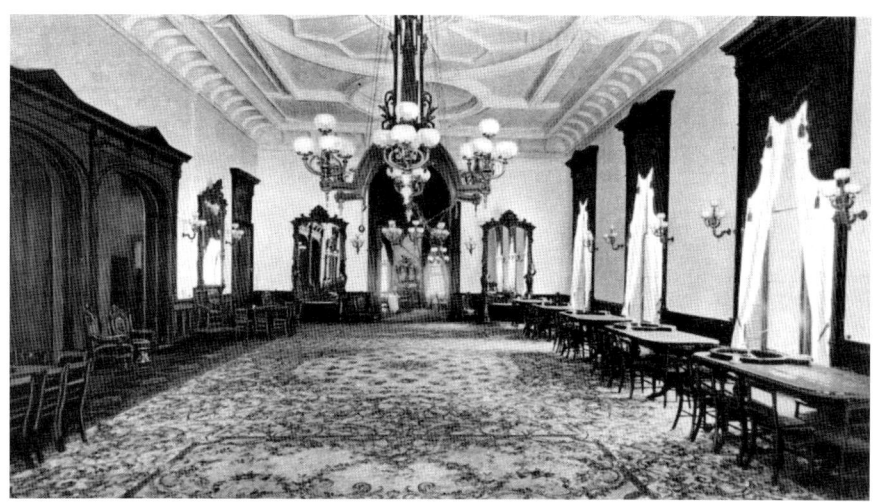

Gaming room at John Morrissey's Saratoga Club House, circa 1875. *George S. Bolster Collection of the Saratoga Springs History Museum.*

building. It was noted that Old Smoke continued offering the pools for several summers in defiance of a law passed by the state legislature, of which he, ironically, had become a member. Predictably, this generated "much comment," according to the *New York Sun*.

The racing at Saratoga in the 1870s was generally considered the finest in America. The Kentucky Derby was first run in 1875, but it was not until the early 1900s that the Run for the Roses and Churchill Downs garnered significant national recognition. Other notable tracks such as Jerome Park and Monmouth Park were also on the scene, among many others, as thoroughbred racing was becoming the country's first national pastime. Saratoga, however, remained the heart and soul of the sport. Several of the decade's finest races took place at Saratoga, including the 1872 Saratoga Cup. In a rematch of the Monmouth Cup from earlier in the summer, Harry Bassett prevailed against a gallant Longfellow, winner of the first meeting. Longfellow suffered a career-ending foot injury during the Saratoga Cup, but he was revered for a heroic effort that came up just short. No other track in America had as many marquee events or elite racehorses as Saratoga did during this time.

As busy as he was with the track and Club House, Morrissey still devoted time to politics. In Congress, he became a close friend of President Andrew Johnson and was well thought of by many, even though his impact was generally regarded as minimal. Following his second term in Congress,

BARE KNUCKLES & SARATOGA RACING

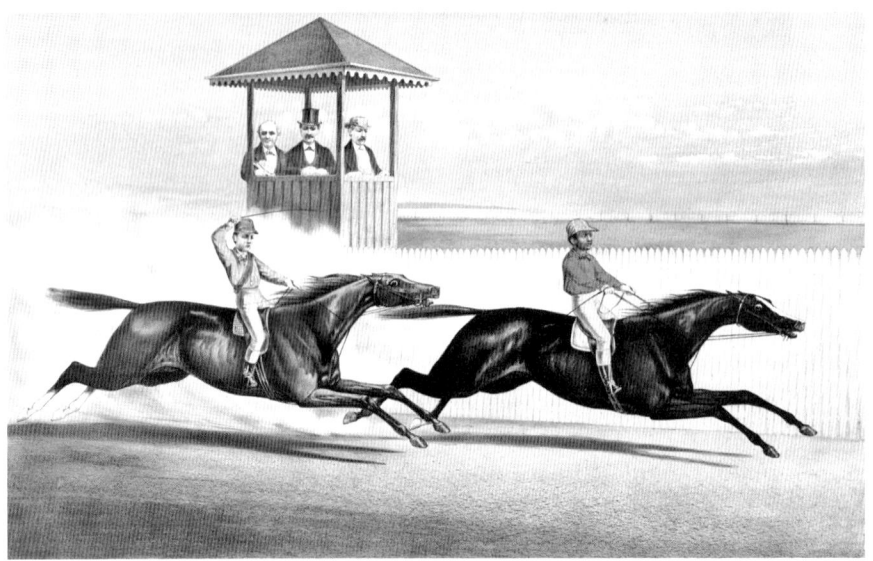

Harry Bassett, *left*, and Longfellow in their famous 1872 Saratoga Cup won by Harry Bassett, from a Currier and Ives print. *Courtesy of the National Museum of Racing and Hall of Fame.*

Morrissey turned his attention back to New York City and Tammany Hall. Boss Tweed and his accomplices were running amok. A faction of the party had seen enough of the corruption and unethical methods that had become accepted practices. In response, Old Smoke helped organize the Young Democracy in an effort to bring down the Tweed Ring. Morrissey's gambling fortune and connection with many of New York's top financiers made him a credible threat to Tammany's stranglehold on the city.

Campaigning on an anti-Tammany platform after being exiled from the organization, Old Smoke made no bones about his disgust for what Tammany had become under Tweed's direction. The organization was bloated at the top with bandits who were stealing as much as $15 million from the city annually. Morrissey, in the *New York Sun*, commented on the city's political issues as investigations into Tammany began:

> *I didn't intend saying anything about it, but as my name has been mentioned by Tweed and the Tammany General Committee's organ, I will answer your question. I think such an exhibition as has been made in the Common Council's chamber in connection with this investigation would not be tolerated by any other country in the world. Just look at it! Here is this man Tweed acknowledging under oath that everyone who did legitimate work for the city from 1861 to 1870 was compelled to pay fifteen per cent*

of the amount of the bills to have them passed by the Board of Supervisors of which he was head; that he made seven-eighths of these men thieves by forcing them to raise their bills fifteen per cent, so that they could pay him and his band the percentage they demanded.

I notice that in his testimony he uses the word "tradesmen." I think that the public would rather have their names, I know one or two of them who have plenty of money. I have in mind one who came from Albany and was the clown of the Ring for a number of years, Tweed also acknowledges that he is the most notorious thief that the world has ever seen, and that no man ever did more to make public officers thieves. Why, the community knows but little of this man's transactions. Rumor says he gave $1,800,000 of the public money to women friends, money he stole from the city treasury. I understand that Wheeler H. Peckham has traced to one of them more than $1,000,000 of the public money. Tweed gallanted her from Maine to California, and through Fifth Avenue and other streets of this city.

The evidence against Tweed began to mount, and so did the opposition, including Morrissey, representing the tip of the spear. Tweed's insatiable greed was his downfall. Political cartoonist Thomas Nast, along with Horace Greeley, owner of the *New York Tribune*, and Samuel J. Tilden, who narrowly won the popular vote in the 1876 presidential election but lost in the House to Rutherford B. Hayes, aligned themselves with Morrissey to bring down Tweed. The combined efforts eventually knocked Tweed from his perch and led to his imprisonment.

A weakened and desperate Tammany Hall attempted to move forward under the new leadership of John Kelly. With the party at a crossroads and in need of some positive public perception, Kelly extended an

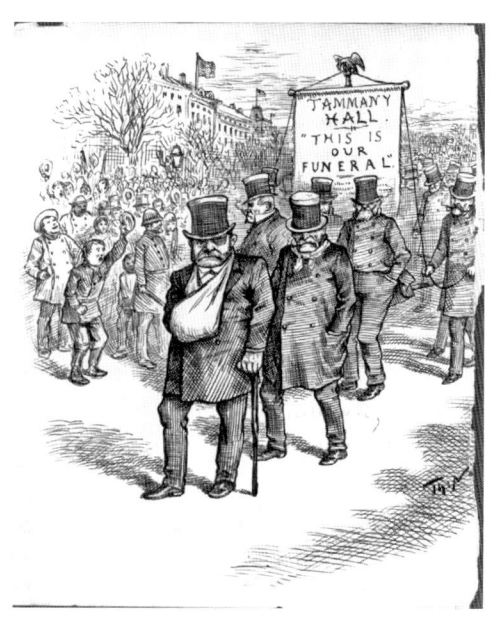

Tammany Hall faced constant accusations of corruption in the nineteenth century. John Morrissey played a key role in the fall of Boss Tweed. *Library of Congress.*

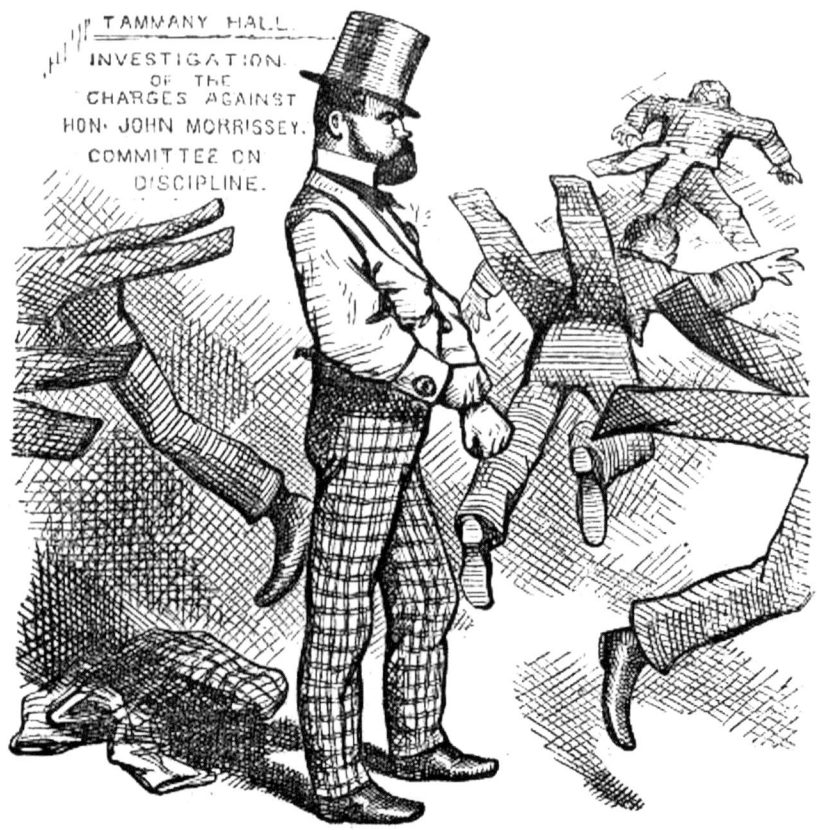

THE "SHORT-HAIR" AND "SWALLOW-TAIL" FIGHT.
Making the "Swallows" Homeward Fly.

A political cartoon depicting John Morrissey's reaction to his expulsion from Tammany Hall. *From* Harper's Weekly.

olive branch to Morrissey and his Young Democracy colleagues in an effort to unify the fractured outfit. Willing to bury the past, Old Smoke accepted reinstatement to Tammany Hall, but the fragile political peace had a short run. Although he wasn't the thief Tweed was, Kelly never fully gained Morrissey's trust, and their relationship quickly eroded. The intraparty battling resumed, and once again the Young Democracy disciples, led by Old Smoke, were kicked out of Tammany. Morrissey had a decisive response for what he believed was political treason on the part of Kelly and his followers.

THE REMARKABLE LIFE OF JOHN MORRISSEY

Old Smoke answered by running for the New York State Senate in 1875 against Tammany Hall's John Fox in the Fourth District. Morrissey won an easy victory and became a major thorn in Tammany's side while serving in Albany. Unlike his time in Congress, Old Smoke was active and influential in this role. He fought every Tammany measure Kelly sponsored and had much success opposing his former party's initiatives. Susie Morrissey attempted to convince her husband to leave politics behind after his first term in Albany. After all, he had the racetrack, the Club House, his New York City gambling interests and all the money he ever needed. It should have been enough to convince Old Smoke to walk away. Morrissey was now in his mid-forties, and perhaps it was time to slow things down a bit.

However, a tragedy may have played a role in Old Smoke continuing in politics. On December 30, 1876, Morrissey's son died at the age of twenty-one from Bright's disease, a severe kidney ailment. John Morrissey Jr. grew up much differently than his father. He was well schooled and a member of a social club. The advantages of his family's wealth allowed him to row in regattas on Saratoga Lake and own trotting horses. He loved to play baseball and by all accounts had a promising future. The death of Morrissey's only child came only two years after Old Smoke's father died in a Troy sanitarium at the age of eighty-five. Maybe another term as a New York State senator would provide at least a minor distraction for Morrissey. Tammany Hall also still needed to be dealt with, and Old Smoke took great pride in making things difficult for his former political allies.

Kelly and the Tammanyites were eager to oust Morrissey from his position in Albany. Old Smoke seemed agreeable to leave on his own, but once he learned that Tammany Hall was planning on endorsing Augustus Schell, the party's former grand sachem, for the Seventh District seat in the 1877 election, Morrissey decided to go one more round in the political ring. Schell was a veteran politician and hailed from one of New York's oldest and most distinguished families. He was an intelligent and formidable opponent, and Old Smoke was considered a long shot in the Seventh District, a longtime Tammany stronghold. Although he had grown tired of the political scene, Morrissey enjoyed the challenge Schell presented and could not resist the competition. He told the *New York Times*:

> *The boys down at the Hall should know me by this time, but I see they don't. The easiest way to have kept me out of Albany was just to say they'd like to have me there. I don't want to go. But when they try to beat me with a white headed old fool, who ought to be in a tulipwood box with silver*

handles, I can't quit. The best fighters in the world couldn't beat me—and Augustus Schell, who couldn't lick his weight in Tabby cats, ain't going to start now!

The campaign against Schell took a significant physical toll on Morrissey. He suffered from bronchitis and was advised by physicians to scale back his public appearances or risk developing pneumonia. The autumn nights on the campaign trail were cold and damp, and Old Smoke traveled about in an open carriage, making as many as a half dozen speeches a night. The contentious campaign was grueling, and both candidates had their share of supporters. Attempting to discredit his opponent, Schell repeatedly charged that Morrissey was once paymaster for the Tweed Ring and dispensed hundreds of thousands of dollars in illegal deals that benefited Tammany's leadership. Old Smoke addressed the allegations with honesty and squashed the matter before it could hinder his prospects. Morrissey told the *New York Times*:

Of course, I did. Every man wants to feather his nest. There ain't a person within the sound of my voice that wouldn't have done the same. I'm no angel, but the things that gang did turned my stomach. I'm fighting them now as hard as I fought for them. That's to your advantage. They haven't changed any. You all know that I never struck a foul blow or turned a card. My word is as good as my bond…I'm not afraid of any man or every man in Tammany Hall.

Old Smoke's health continued to decline. Doctors ordered him to stay in bed and rest as the campaign reached its final days. The essential work had been completed, and all there was to do was wait. On the night of the election, Morrissey was home in bed when the results became official. He had won another fight. Old Smoke defeated his Tammany adversary Schell for the New York State Senate seat from the Seventh District and struck another blow against his former party. It proved to be Morrissey's final grand victory.

Following the election, Old Smoke's condition worsened. His throat was in great pain, and the top doctors in New York didn't have any answers of substance. It was suggested that he travel south to get away from the cold and damp conditions in the city. Senator Morrissey and his wife took the advice and traveled to Savannah, Georgia, by private train on November 16, 1857. Old Smoke had a doctor and nurse by his side at every moment. The Morrisseys stayed in Savannah for several weeks before moving on to Jacksonville, Florida. Old Smoke's condition was not improving, and he grew

THE REMARKABLE LIFE OF JOHN MORRISSEY

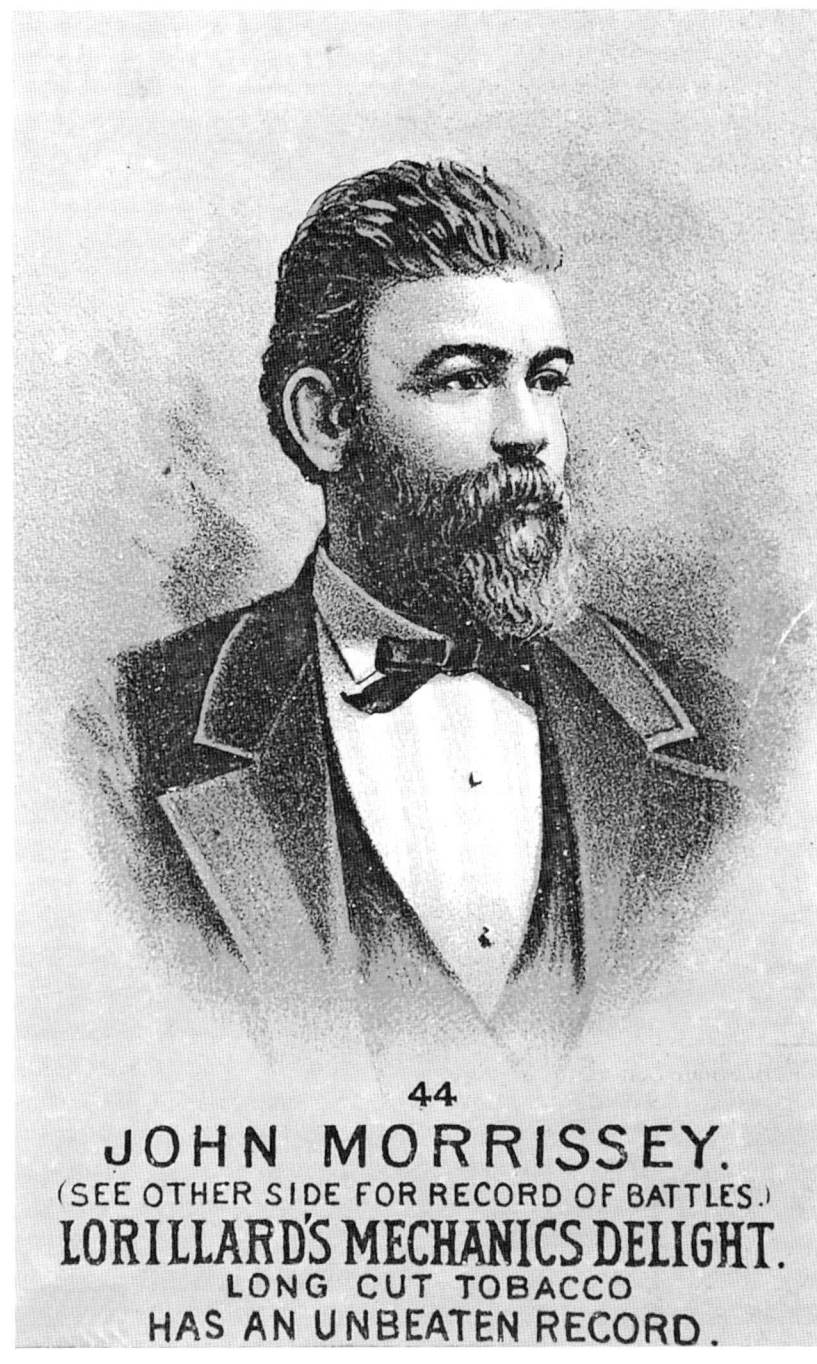

John Morrissey, from a nineteenth-century tobacco card. *Courtesy of a private collection.*

frustrated. Morrissey bristled at the solitude around him. He had always been a man of action and adventure. He craved the crowds and the action at Saratoga Race Course. He missed the whirling roulette wheels at the Club House and the hustle and bustle of New York City. He had grown tired of politics, but even the halls and floor of the Senate in Albany appealed to him more than the monotonous and sleepy southern experience.

After spending the winter in Florida, John and Susie Morrissey returned to New York via steamship in late March 1878. Old Smoke began to show some improvement, and there was hope for a recovery. Upon his return, the *New York Herald* said Morrissey's face "had a healthy glow, and he walked down the gangplank with a firm and steady step." After only a day in New York, Old Smoke took a boat to Troy, caught a cold and suffered a severe relapse into his prior condition.

On April 19, Morrissey was taken to Saratoga and set up in a private room in the new Adelphi Hotel. He again showed signs of a recovery and by all accounts was eager to get back to business. He had work to do in Albany and yearned to be among the gamblers at the Club House and at Saratoga Race Course. In only a few months, racing would return to the track Old Smoke built and so expertly presided over. He looked forward to the elegant procession of rumbling hoofs and the beauty and pageantry of the summer season at Saratoga.

Senator Morrissey, however, never saw the majestic horses at the track again. He never played another game of poker at the Club House. He never returned to Albany. In late April 1878, Old Smoke suffered a stroke that cost him the use of his right arm and confined him to his bed at the Adelphi. A fever dogged him, his breathing was laborious and his face was colorless and drawn. The *New York Tribune* quoted Morrissey as saying, "I'm running neck and neck with death, and rapidly tiring." Knowing the end was near, Morrissey added, "Yes, I am a gambler and a prizefighter, but no man can ever say that I turned a dishonest card or struck a foul blow."

Death took John Morrissey at seven-thirty in the evening of May 1, 1878. With his wife and several friends and employees at his bedside, Old Smoke closed his eyes for the final time while clasping the hand of a priest in his room at the Adelphi Hotel. He was forty-seven years old.

Epilogue
THE LEGACY OF OLD SMOKE

John Morrissey's death was the lead story in every New York City paper on May 2, 1878. The flag at city hall was lowered to half-staff, the senate in Albany adjourned to mourn the loss of their colleague and, in a rare tribute, play was suspended on the gambling tables at 5 West Twenty-fourth Street in New York City. The papers all acknowledged Old Smoke's unique imprint. The *New York Times* said Morrissey's death was "a loss to the cause of good government in New York" and added that "no man ever charged John Morrissey with being a venal legislator or a dishonest politician." The *New York Tribune* said he "had a good deal of the prize-fighter's respect for fair play and the bruiser's brute courage" and believed "that workingmen—with whom he had nothing whatever in common—ought somehow to get a living out of the public treasury." *Harper's Weekly* called him "a man of strict integrity."

The *Spirit of the Times*, the leading sporting publication of the era, perhaps stated it best in acknowledging that Old Smoke "left a deep and peculiar stamp upon his time" and was "something akin to genius" as an entrepreneur and sportsman. The *Spirit* praised his various talents, sense of purpose and resolve, as well as his "generosity almost to a fault when he believed anyone was worthy of it." It added that his death would "draw regrets from tens of thousands who never saw him."

More than fifteen thousand people attended Morrissey's funeral on a rainy spring day in Troy. The entire state senate attended. "No burial ever evoked so many emotions of sorrow from the mass of the people—the hard, rough workingmen and women," reported the *New York Times*. "They tuned

EPILOGUE

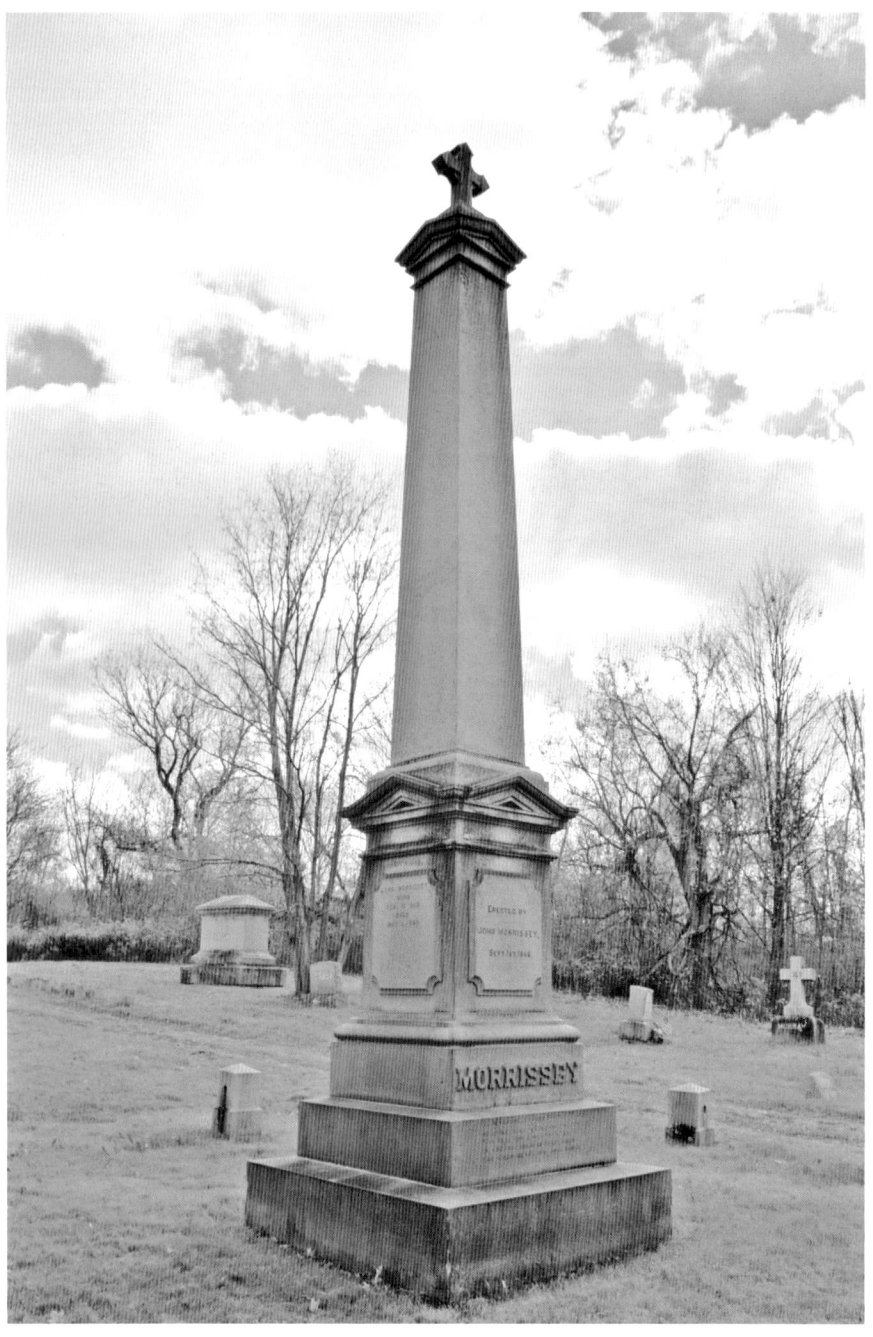

John Morrissey's grave at St. Peter's Cemetery, Troy, New York. *Brien Bouyea photo*.

EPILOGUE

out en masse today, in their working clothes and with grit upon their faces, to watch with tears in their eyes the passage of the funeral procession."

As the soft rain fell, John Morrissey was buried in St. Peter's Cemetery in Troy. There was seldom a dull moment in his forty-seven years. He was a man of achievement and distinction. He rose above what his lineage suggested he would become and was an example that pure ambition was a trait that could take a man to great heights. Old Smoke was a product of his times, becoming a hard man out of necessity and using his fists as a means to an end. They served him well in what became a prosperous life to the end.

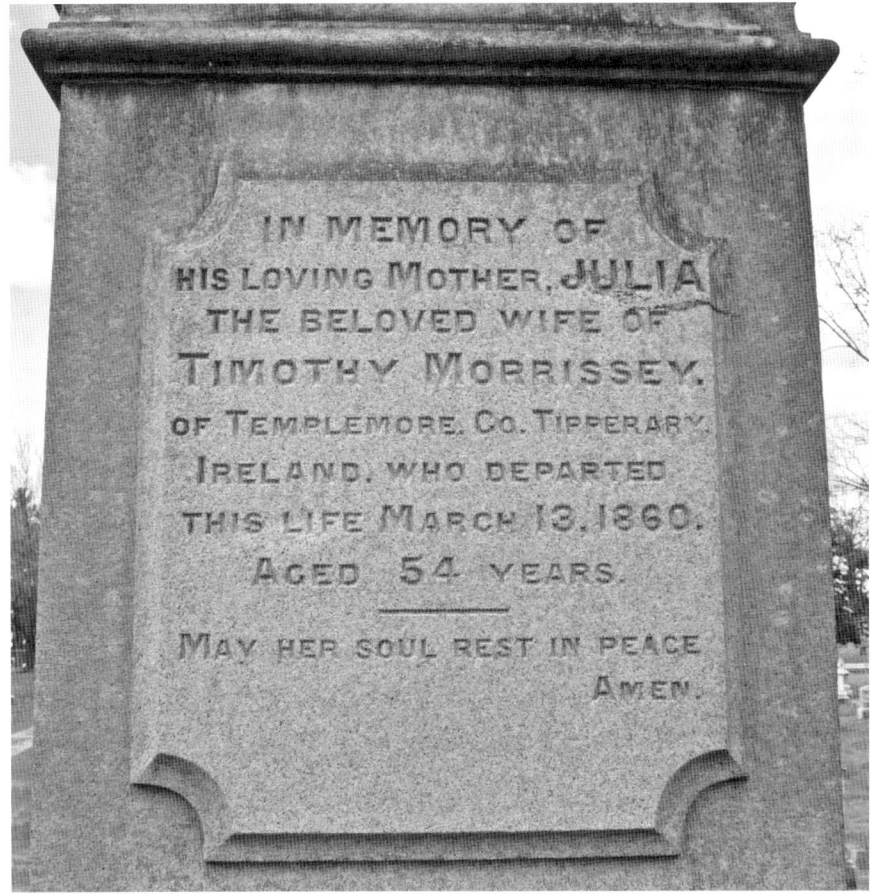

Detail of the Morrissey family monument at St. Peter's Cemetery, Troy, New York. *Brien Bouyea photo*.

EPILOGUE

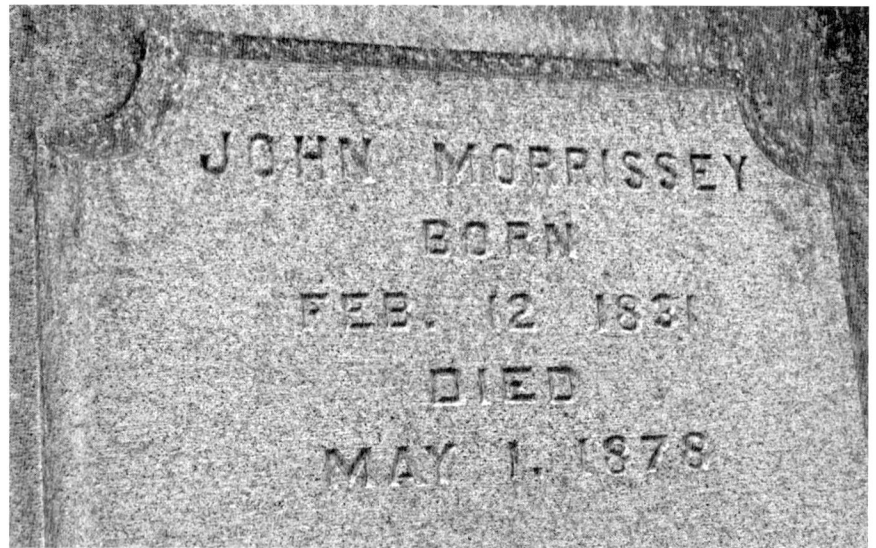

Detail of the Morrissey family monument at St. Peter's Cemetery, Troy, New York. *Brien Bouyea photo*.

Many of Morrissey's contemporaries were not as fortunate. Following his loss to Old Smoke in 1853, Yankee Sullivan made his way to California and became a disgraced shoulder hitter. Sullivan was the guard of a ballot box in San Francisco that was tampered with and resulted in the election of James P. Casey to a city office despite Casey not even being on the ballot. After Casey murdered a journalist for exposing his criminal background, vigilantes seized power in the city and arrested Casey and Sullivan for election fraud. At trial, Sullivan was sentenced to deportation for his role in the matter. On May 31, 1856, Sullivan was found dead in his jail cell. The main artery in his left arm had been severed by a razor. His death was ruled a suicide, but some accounts claimed that Sullivan's enemies murdered him.

After fighting Tom Sayers to a draw in England in 1860, John Heenan contested one more bare-knuckle bout, losing a controversial fight on English soil against Tom King in December 1863. After much success early in the fight, Heenan faded badly and was defeated in the twenty-fourth round. Many observers were adamant that King received favorable treatment from the referee throughout the fight and had been given more time than the rules allowed to recover from a knockdown in the eighteenth round. Heenan unexplainably collapsed six rounds later and could not continue. It was speculated that he had somehow been drugged. The Benicia Boy returned to America in 1865 and attempted to enter the gambling business. His luck

EPILOGUE

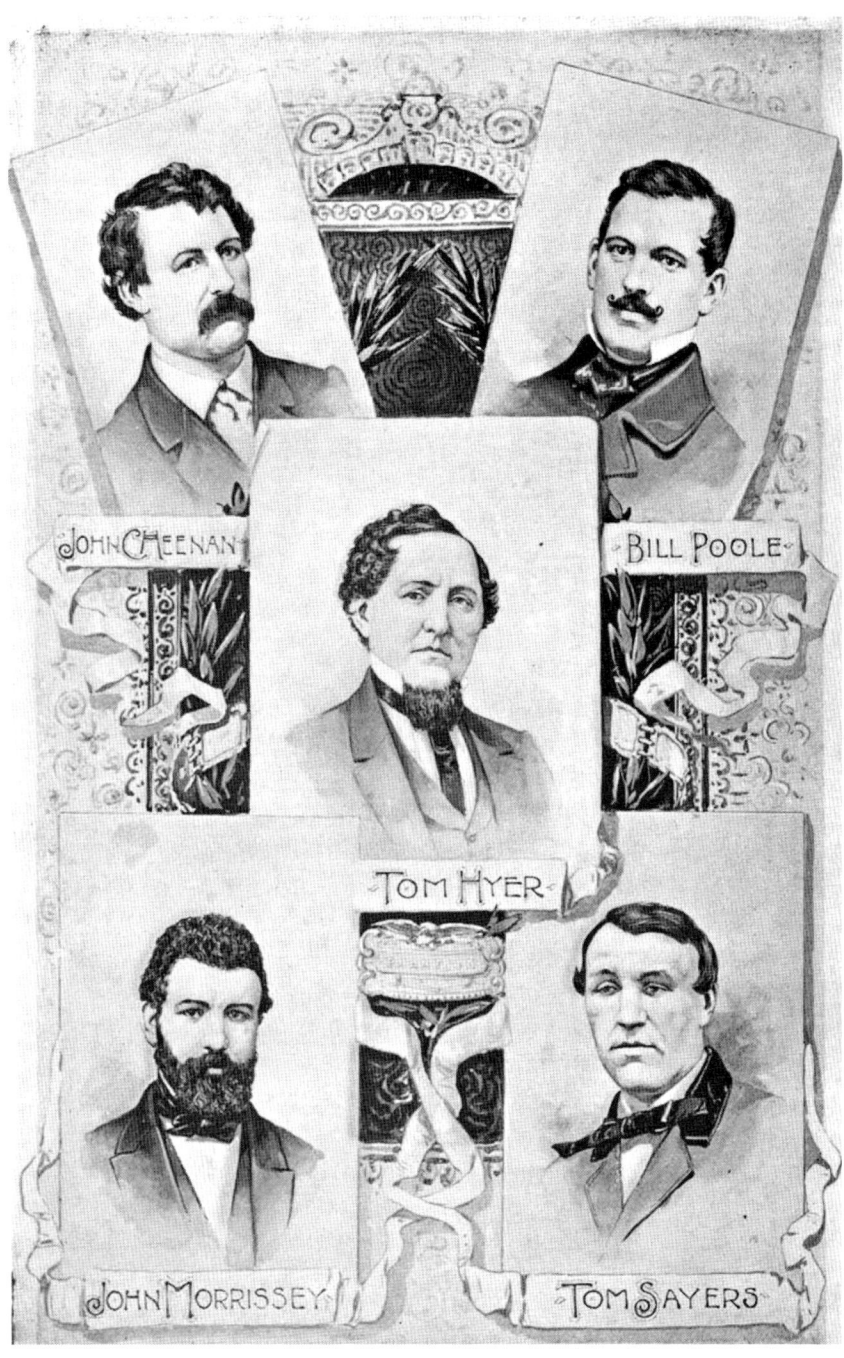

A nineteenth-century illustration of famous fighters John Heenan, Bill Poole, Tom Sayers, Tom Hyer and John Morrissey. *Courtesy of a private collection.*

EPILOGUE

went from bad to worse, and he eventually developed tuberculosis. In hopes that the supposedly pure western air would help him recover, Heenan went to Green River Station in the Wyoming Territory in 1873. He died there shortly after his arrival at the age of thirty-nine. Jim Cusick, Heenan's old trainer and loyal friend, also made the journey to Wyoming and was with him at the end. He took Heenan's body back to New York and made sure the Benicia Boy received a proper burial in St. Agnes Cemetery in Albany.

Morrissey's adversaries among the Know-Nothings fared no better. Bill Poole was just thirty-three when Lew Baker killed him in 1855, and Tom Hyer died a drunken beggar at the age of forty-five in 1864. Boss Tweed, meanwhile, managed to escape from prison and flee to Spain. He was later captured and returned to New York City. He died at the age of fifty-five after contracting severe pneumonia while a federal prisoner in New York's Ludlow Street Jail. Tweed died only three weeks prior to Old Smoke.

Upon Morrissey's death, ownership of the Club House and a controlling interest in Saratoga Race Course passed to Albert Spencer and Charles Reed, a couple of Old Smoke's former New York City gambling partners. They eventually sold the Club House to the infamous gambler Richard Canfield for $250,000 in 1883. Canfield reportedly spent an additional $800,000 to further enhance the facility and grounds in a more European style. In the Canfield era, the venue was as popular and profitable as any casino in the world until anti-gambling crusaders attained considerable power in the early 1900s. Canfield was forced to shut down the operation for good in 1907 and sold the venue to the Village of Saratoga Springs in 1911 for less than the original purchase price. The building is now home to the Saratoga Springs History Museum and has been recognized as a National Historic Landmark. Old Smoke's portrait from the 1870s remains a proud fixture on the museum's second floor.

Although politics occupied much of his time during his final years, Morrissey maintained a prominent role at Saratoga Race Course until the time of his death. Without its founder, the track sustained its reputation as one of America's premier sports venues through the 1880s with Reed and Spencer at the helm before troubled times arrived in the final decade of the century. The Saratoga Association honored Old Smoke with the running of the Morrissey Stakes each year from 1881 through 1894. The 1890s, however, proved to be a dark time for racing at Saratoga. The track's early stalwarts—Morrissey, William Travers, Leonard Jerome and Commodore Vanderbilt—had all died, and the new management at Saratoga left a lot to be desired following Reed and Spencer. Other key players from the

EPILOGUE

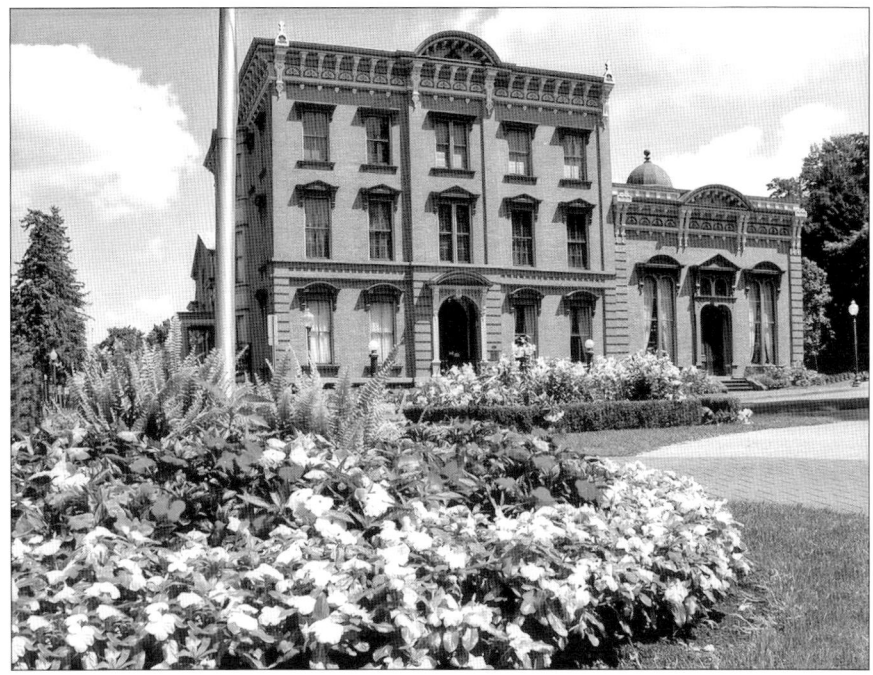

John Morrissey's former Club House is now home to the Saratoga Springs History Museum. *Brien Bouyea photo.*

track's formative years were no longer fixtures. James Marvin resigned from the Saratoga Association at the age of eighty-two, and Charles Wheatly, who helped design the track and served more than three decades as racing secretary, also moved on.

In their wake, Gottfried Walbaum took over as the track's operator in 1892. A former brothel owner, Walbaum operated the Guttenberg track in New Jersey, and his success there resulted in daily profits in excess of $5,000, but his management was not without controversy. In 1891, Walbaum was indicted in New Jersey for activities relating to Guttenberg. The *New York Times* reported, "The Hudson County Grand Jury, in their batch of indictments handed to Judge Knapp on Thursday night, included one against Gottfried Walbaum, President of the Hudson County Jockey Club, for keeping a 'disorderly house' at the Guttenberg race track, and against James Brown and Edward Shapley for selling pools at the track."

Walbaum was despised in Saratoga from the beginning. He infuriated hotel owners and visitors alike when he moved the start of racing from its customary time of 11:30 a.m. to 2:30 p.m. simply because he enjoyed

EPILOGUE

gambling deep into the night and was disinclined to get up before noon. Saratoga's attendance and handle suffered greatly, and Walbaum did not seem to care. He further rankled traditionalists when he allowed women and children to openly gamble, prompting journalist Nellie Bly to condone Saratoga as "the wickedest spot in the United States." Walbaum provided "retiring rooms" in the grandstand where bookmakers and ticket sellers took bets from women and children. Walbaum made no attempt to hide what was going on. "Wild Vortex of Gambling and Betting by Men, Women and Children" and "Sports, Touts, Criminals and Race-Track Riff-Raff Crazed by the Mania for Gold" were among the headlines of stories with Saratoga datelines published by the *New York World* in 1894.

In his book *Saratoga: Saga of an Impious Era*, George Waller said Walbaum "had come to the Springs with virtually nothing to recommend him. He was boastful and profane, a gambler, bookmaker and, it was said, had once run a brothel; it was also claimed that at the Guttenberg race track in New Jersey, which he had owned, horses had been stimulated with electric shocks to make them run faster. Under his management the Saratoga track had none of the elegance Canfield brought to the Club House. It was a haven for touts and thieves; and the races were so flagrantly dishonest that the better stables refused to participate."

Morrissey was no saint, but his leadership, business acumen and ability to provide quality racing and a genteel environment keyed Saratoga Race Course's early success. The pits of the Walbaum era illustrated just how much Old Smoke was missed.

While Walbaum initially turned a profit at Saratoga, the quality of the racing deteriorated quickly on his watch. In response to the track's overall decline, many prominent stables abandoned racing at Saratoga and refused to return until new management took over. Several of the signature races that had risen to national prominence in the Morrissey era and later in the 1880s—the Saratoga Cup, Travers Stakes, Alabama Stakes and Spinaway Stakes among them—were either suspended or saw significant purse reductions under Walbaum. The Travers, the famed fixture that dated back to opening day in 1864, saw its purse sliced to a pitiful $1,125 in 1895.

Things were so bad that in 1896 Saratoga Race Course didn't open at all. Walbaum was finally forced into a lesser profile the following year when the track reopened, but Saratoga racing struggled until William Collins Whitney arrived on the scene to lead a syndicate that revitalized the track at the turn of the century. The major races were reinstated, purses rose and needed improvements were made throughout the property. Saratoga

EPILOGUE

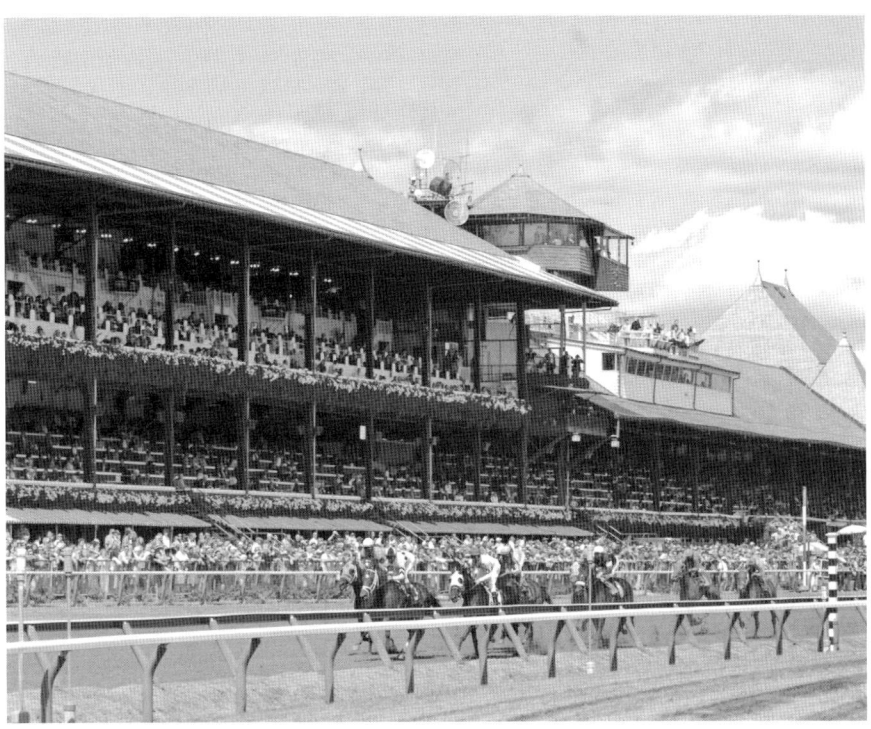

Saratoga Race Course during the 2015 season. *New York Racing Association*.

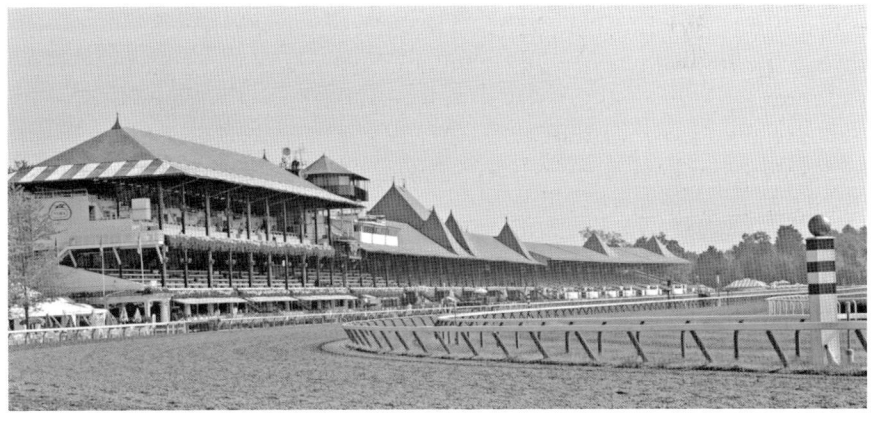

Saratoga Race Course, the oldest active sporting venue in America. *New York Racing Association*.

EPILOGUE

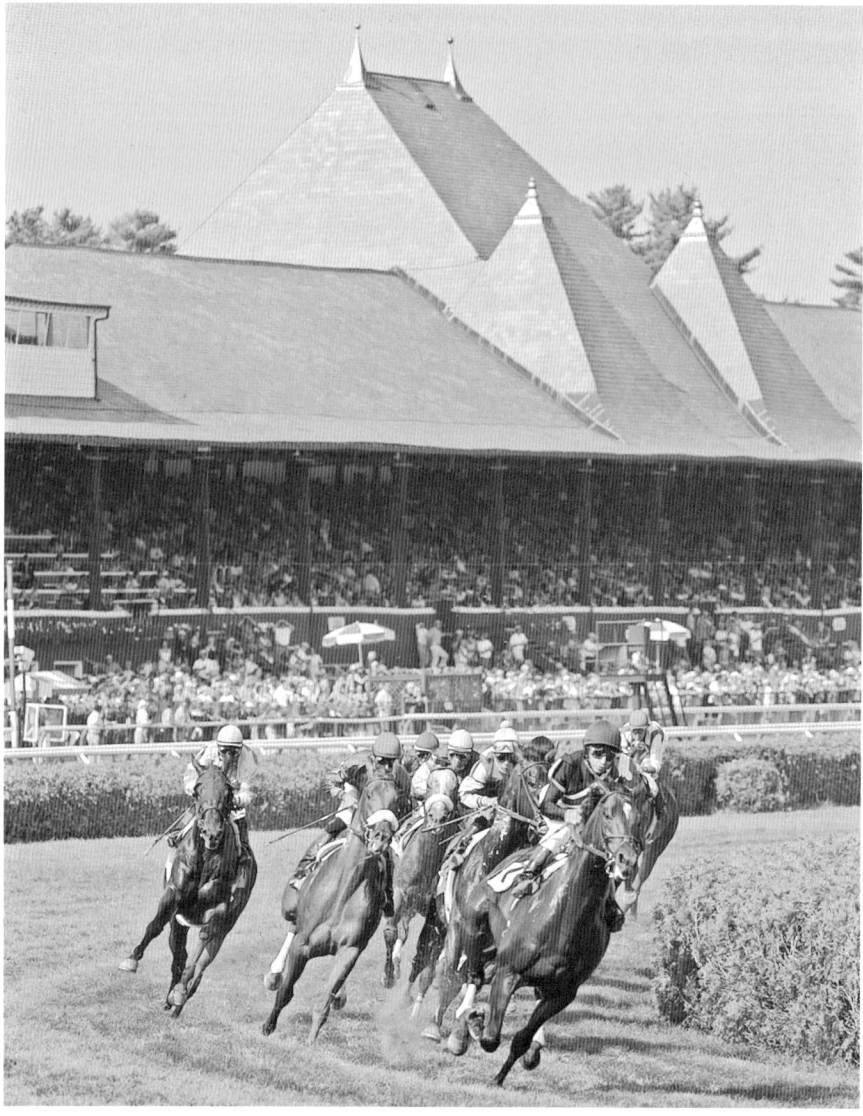

Saratoga Race Course was selected by *Sports Illustrated* as one of the top ten sporting venues in the world. *New York Racing Association*.

racing had returned to elite status, and thanks in large part to Whitney, John Morrissey's creation would endure as one of America's greatest sporting treasures.

Old Smoke finally received some long-overdue recognition for his contributions to thoroughbred racing when the New York Racing Association

EPILOGUE

corrected an oversight in its Saratoga stakes schedule and inaugurated the John Morrissey Stakes for New York–breds in 2004. In 2013, the Saratoga Springs community and its summer patrons celebrated the 150th anniversary of Morrissey's 1863 meeting with a series of special events at the track and throughout town.

Boxing historians at long last got around to recognizing Morrissey's fistic achievements and unblemished ring record with induction into the International Boxing Hall of Fame in Canastota, New York, in 1996. Six years after Old Smoke's induction as a pioneer of the rugged bare-knuckle era, his old rival John Heenan was elected to the Hall of Fame. Tom Hyer, who never seemed to want anything to do with Morrissey in the ring, was enshrined in 2009.

Old Smoke was a lot of things in life. He didn't learn to read and write until he was nineteen, but sixteen years later he was a national sensation thanks to his improbable election to the United States House of Representatives. In the adventurous time between, Morrissey led the dreaded Dead Rabbits into bloody New York City street wars with the Know-Nothings, became one of America's most famous gamblers and reigned as American boxing champion. He never lost in the ring and was even more successful outside it. He improbably resurrected thoroughbred racing in America and built the sport's greatest venue in Saratoga against the backdrop of the Civil War, something for which he deserves considerably more credit than he generally receives.

In the more expansive history of the volatile times in which he existed and thrived, John Morrissey's legacy is a mere footnote, but that in no way diminishes his extraordinary story or various successes. Old Smoke stood out as a unique figure because of insatiable ambition that was always followed by swift and decisive action en route to achieving his objectives.

Above all else, it was simply a life well lived, worthy of remembrance and respect.

BIBLIOGRAPHY

Ackerman, Kenneth D. *Boss Tweed: The Corrupt Pol Who Conceived the Soul of Modern New York*. N.p.: Viral History Press, 2011.

Asbury, Herbert. *The Gangs of New York*. Garden City, NY: Garden City Publishing Co., 1928.

Bartels, Jon. *Saratoga Stories: Gangsters, Gamblers & Racing Legends*. Lexington, KY: Eclipse Press, 2007.

Bradley, Hugh. *Such Was Saratoga*. New York: Doubleday, Doran and Co., 1940.

Gorn, Elliott J. *The Manly Art: Bare-Knuckle Prize Fighting in America*. Ithaca, NY: Cornell University Press, 1986.

Harding, William E. *John Morrissey: His Life, Battles and Wrangles*. New York: Richard K. Fox Co., 1881.

Hotaling, Edward. *They're Off! Horse Racing at Saratoga*. Syracuse, NY: Syracuse University Press, 1995.

Kofoed, Jack. *Brandy for Heroes*. New York: E.P. Dutton and Co., 1938.

Lane, Wheaton J. *Commodore Vanderbilt: An Epic of the Steam Age*. New York: Knopf, 1942.

Leslie, Anita. *The Remarkable Mr. Jerome*. New York: Henry Holt and Co., 1954.

Manning, Landon. *The Noble Animals: Tales of the Saratoga Turf*. Saratoga Springs, NY: self-published, 1973.

Riess, Steven A. *The Sport of Kings and the Kings of Crime*. Syracuse, NY: Syracuse University Press, 2011.

Sandburg, Carl. *Abraham Lincoln: The War Years*. New York: Harcourt, Brace and Co., 1926.

BIBLIOGRAPHY

Veitch, Michael. *Foundations of Fame: Nineteenth Century Thoroughbred Racing in Saratoga Springs.* Saratoga Springs, NY: Advantage Press, 2004.
Vosburgh, Walter. *Racing in America, 1866–1921.* New York: Scribner Press, 1922.
Waller, George. *Saratoga: Saga of an Impious Era.* Englewood Cliffs, NJ: Prentice Hall, 1966.

PERIODICALS

Albany Evening Journal
Brooklyn Eagle
Chicago Daily Tribune
Daily Saratogian
Frank Leslie's Illustrated Newspaper
LaCrosse Democrat
New York Clipper
New York Daily Tribune
New York Sun
New York Times
New York World
Police Gazette
Saratoga Republican
Troy Record
Troy Times
Wilkes' Spirit of the Times

INDEX

A

Abbey Hotel 79
Adams, John Quincy 88
Adelphi Hotel 122
Alabama Stakes 130
Albany 18, 19, 119, 122, 123, 128
Allaire, Charley 56, 59, 60
Allen, Theodore 68, 75
Americus Club 23, 24, 26, 31, 38, 45, 48, 51
Annieswood Stable 100
Appomattox Courthouse 103
Arthur, Chester A. 113
Astor House 42

B

Baker, Hamilton 113
Baker, Lew 73, 75, 84, 128
Barbee, George 105
Barhyte, Jacobus 89
Battle of Gettysburg 89
Beasley, Tom 23
Bird, William 97
Bly, Nellie 130
Boston 96
Boston Corners 54, 55, 56, 60, 61
Botany Bay 54
Broeck, Richard Ten 96
Broughton, Jack 46
Brown, Edward 105
Buchanan 97
Bull's Head Tavern 64
Burch, William 105
Burgoyne, Billy 95
Burgoyne, John 87
Burns, Tom 24, 28

C

Canfield, Richard 128
Captain Moore 95, 96, 97
Casey, James P. 126
Churchill Downs 115
Churchill, Winston 98
City of Troy 19, 20, 26, 42, 63
Civil War 89, 95, 102, 103, 111, 133
Clay, Henry 94
Clay, John 94
Club House 113, 114, 115, 119, 122, 128, 130
Coburn, Joe 77
Cole, George 91
Congress Hall 89

INDEX

Congress Park 113, 114
Cooper, James Fenimore 88
Corning, Erastus 100
Cunningham, Daniel "Dad" 43, 64, 75, 84
Cusick, Jim 77, 128

D

Daly, "One Eye" 25, 28
Danser, Matt 84
Davidson, John B. 100
Dead Rabbits 34, 52, 65, 76, 85, 91, 133
Draft Riots 89
Duane, "Dutch Charley" 25
Duke of Magenta 105

E

Eddy, John 100
Emperor of Norfolk 105

F

Five Points 33, 34
Fox, John 119

G

Gardner, Orville "Awful" 56, 57, 60, 84
Garryowen 103
Gettysburg 95
Girard House 64, 65
Goodhue, Jonathan 88
Gould, Jay 113
Grand Union Hotel 89
Grant, Ulysses S. 103, 106, 113
Greeley, Horace 117

H

Hall, A. Oakley 65
Hamilton, Alex 17, 20, 23, 24, 28, 36
Hamilton, Jack "Shepherd" 79
Harlem Railroad 55, 107
Harry Bassett 105, 115
Hayes, Rutherford B. 113, 117

Heenan, John Camel "Benicia Boy" 77, 81, 82, 83, 86, 126, 133
Hindoo 105
Hudson River 15, 16, 19
Hughes, Lloyd 105
Hunter, John R. 98
Hyer, Jacob 23
Hyer, Tom 23, 25, 36, 44, 48, 49, 51, 53, 61, 76, 128, 133

I

International Boxing Hall of Fame 133
Irving, Washington 88

J

James, Ed 70
Jerome, Leonard 89, 98, 100, 128
Jerome Park 98, 115
Jersey Derby 102
Jockey Club, the 100
John Morgan 97
John Morrissey Stakes 133
Johnson, Andrew 115

K

Kelly, John 117
Kennedy, John A. 52
Kentucky 102, 103, 104
Kentucky Derby 97, 115
Kingsland, Ambrose 53
King, Tom 126
Know-Nothings 24, 28, 31, 32, 34, 35, 36, 45, 51, 65, 68, 128

L

Lady Digby 92
Lady Suffolk 26, 91, 92, 95
Lansingburgh 79
Lee, Robert E. 103
Lexington 96, 102
Lilly, Christopher 54
Lincoln, Abraham 89, 97, 105
Lizzie W. 95, 96, 97

INDEX

Longfellow 105, 115
Long Point Island 79, 80
Lozier, Charley 73
Luke Blackburn 105
Lyng, Johnny 70

M

Mackey, John 20
Mare Island 44, 46
Marvin, James 91, 100, 129
McCann, Tom 35, 36, 37, 38, 40, 41, 42
McCloskey, George "Country" 23
McCoy, Thomas 54
McGrath, Henry Price 97
McGrathiana Stud 97
McLaughlin, James 105
McLaughlin, Paugeen 73, 75
M'Geehan, Bibber 18
Miss Woodford 105
Monmouth Cup 115
Monmouth Park 115
Morris, Robert 54
Morrissey, John, Jr. 76, 119
Morrissey, Julia 14, 85, 86
Morrissey, Susie 76, 79, 122
Morrissey, Tim 14, 86
Morse, Samuel 32
Moscow 92
Murphy, Isaac 105

N

Nast, Thomas 117
National Museum of Racing and Hall of Fame 103
New York City 14, 15, 16, 19, 20, 23, 42, 54, 67, 84, 89, 109, 116, 123, 128
New York Racing Association 132

O

O'Donnell, Tom 56, 60
O'Rourke, John 20
Osgood, George 100

P

Pacific Steamship Company 77
Parole 105
Patrick, Gilbert Watson 96
Patten, Alfonso 91
Petrie, John 41, 42, 44, 63, 64, 84
Pimlico Race Course 100
Pincus, Jacob 105
Poe, Edgar Allan 89
Poole, William "Bill the Butcher" 24, 26, 28, 36, 45, 51, 52, 53, 57, 68, 73, 75, 128
Prioress 96
Purdy, John 100

R

Reed, Charles 128
Revolutionary War 88, 89
Ridgely, Kate 36, 37
Rockefeller, John 113
Ruthless 105
Rynders, Isaiah 24, 28, 31, 32, 51

S

San Francisco 43, 44, 126
Saratoga Association for the Improvement of the Breed of Horses 103
Saratoga Cup 103, 104, 115, 130
Saratoga Lake 88, 119
Saratoga Race Course 102, 103, 105, 107, 113, 114, 122, 128, 130
Saratoga Springs 87, 89, 91, 95, 114, 122, 128, 133
Saratoga Springs History Museum 128
Saratoga Trotting Course 91, 93, 95, 100, 101
Sayers, Tom 86, 126
Schell, Augustus 67, 119, 120
Sequel Stakes 102
Seven Oaks 97
Seward, William H. 51
Sewell 95, 97
Shay, Cy 73

139

INDEX

Sheehan, Andy 57, 60
Sheridan, Philip 106
Sherman, William Tecumseh 106
Smith, Captain Levi 19, 20, 21, 42, 63
Smith, Edmund Kirby 94
Smith, Susie 20, 21, 32, 37, 63, 65. *See also* Morrissey, Susie
Spencer, Albert 128
Spinaway Stakes 130
Stanwix Hall 71, 75
Stewart, A.T. 88
St. James Hotel 37, 38
St. Peter's Cemetery 125
Sullivan, Yankee 23, 44, 53, 54, 57, 60, 61, 63, 77, 81, 126
Sympathy 96, 97

T

Tammany Hall 24, 28, 34, 51, 65, 67, 100, 105, 107, 109, 111, 116, 117, 118, 119
Templemore 14, 15, 16
Thompson, George 44, 58
Tilden, Samuel J. 117
Tipperary 102, 103
Travers Stakes 102, 130
Travers, William 98, 128
Troy 14, 15, 16, 17, 19, 20, 21, 26, 32, 56, 65, 77, 79, 85, 122, 123, 125
Turner, Jim 73, 75
Twain, Mark 113
Tweed, William Magear "Boss" 109, 116, 128
Tyler, John 92

U

Underwood, Dr. Robert 97
United States Hotel 89

V

Van Buren, Martin 92
Vanderbilt, Cornelius "Commodore" 84, 85, 98, 107, 113, 128
Vicksburg 95

W

Walbaum, Gottfried 129
Walden, R.W. 105
Washington, George 88
Weldon, Dr. J.W. 96
Wheatly, Charles 100, 129
White, John 100
Whitney, William Collins 130
Williamson, Ansel 105
Wilson, "Admiral Billy" 57, 60
Wilson, Samuel 15
Wood, Ben 85
Wood, Fernando 49, 52, 53, 67, 68, 84, 111

Y

Young Democracy 116, 118

ABOUT THE AUTHOR

Brien Bouyea is director of communications at the National Museum of Racing and Hall of Fame in Saratoga Springs, New York, a positon he has held since 2010. Prior to joining the museum, he was an award-winning sportswriter for the *Record* (Troy, New York) and executive sports editor for the *Saratogian* (Saratoga Springs, New York). His writing awards include national honors from the Associated Press Sports Editors, as well as the New York State Associated Press and the New York Newspaper Publishers Association. He is a regular contributor to *Saratoga Living* magazine and served on the Saratoga 150 History Committee. A graduate of the College of Saint Rose in Albany, New York, he lives in Saratoga Springs, New York.

Visit us at
www.historypress.net
....
This title is also available as an e-book